How to
Be a Writer

How to
Be a Writer

Baths, Biscuits and Endless Cups of Tea

MARCUS BERKMANN

Little, Brown

LITTLE, BROWN

First published in Great Britain in 2022 by Little, Brown

1 3 5 7 9 10 8 6 4 2

A CIP catalogue record for this book
is available from the British Library.

ISBN 978-1-4087-1383-9

Typeset in Times by M Rules
Printed and bound in Great Britain by Clays Ltd, Elcograf S.p.A.

Papers used by Little, Brown are from well-managed forests
and other responsible sources.

Little, Brown
An imprint of
Little, Brown Book Group
Carmelite House
50 Victoria Embankment
London EC4Y 0DZ

An Hachette UK Company
www.hachette.co.uk

www.littlebrown.co.uk

To Amanda, Kate and Jane, with love and thanks

Contents

Introduction

'Journalism is the only job that requires no degrees, no diplomas and no specialised knowledge of any kind.'

Patrick Campbell

I have been a freelance writer since 26 June 1988, when I was twenty-seven. I had left my last real job the day before, in some relief, having decided that the longer I could avoid having to get another real job, the happier I would be. Some people are suited to office life, with its endless meetings, its stationery cupboards and the huge, never-ending task of trying to destroy your rivals' careers. But it wasn't for me. I had been working for a kids' computer magazine, which was excellent training for a writing life – we had to churn the words out, as though on a production line – but poor for mental and physical health. Never, before or since, have I drunk as much lager as I did in the eighteen months I was there. It was three pints at lunchtime and vats of the stuff in the evening, with a shocking hangover in the morning and a large bottle of Lucozade before I could even hope to function. But although I was banging out words by the tens of thousands every week, I was also earning more in the evenings and at the weekend from my freelance career, so it was time to move on. I have never looked back, until now.

This book has come about for two reasons. One is that, in the intervening years, I have written untold millions of words, and for a long time I wondered whether any of them were any good. A friend of mine, a much more eminent writer than I, told me a while ago that he had started putting together a greatest hits of journalism, only to find that even his best stuff simply wasn't up to scratch. But he has always dashed off his journalism, proud of his ability to produce a thousand words in less than an hour and earn hundreds of pounds while I was probably staring out of the window, eating biscuits. His books, he says, are the real work, sweated over and forged in the white-hot crucible of his creativity. I am less fluent and have always had to work hard on everything I do. I'm not sure my books are as good as his, but I thought my journalism might be better. Writing and compiling this book seemed a good way of finding out.

The other reason is that non-writers and aspiring writers have often asked me how I got started, how my career has panned out, what it's like doing what I do. People are intrigued by writers' lives, even the lives of jobbing craftsmen like me who can't believe that they have managed to keep going, doing something they love, for as long as they have. We read all the time about the lives of great writers, thinking their magnificent, beautiful thoughts while lying on chaises longues and eating grapes, pausing only to dash off a few words of brilliance before rushing out to address the Royal Society. Whereas I sit in a first-and-second-floor maisonette in north London, far too small for the four of us who live here, pausing occasionally to do the washing-up. I write mainly in the morning, usually in my dressing gown, because I'm too idle and distracted to get dressed. I should probably admit here that I own more dressing gowns than suits, by a score of three to two. (A thick one for winter, a thin one for summer, an intermediate one for autumn and spring.)

So on the face of it, this has been a deeply boring life, in which almost nothing has happened: a bit like most people's in that respect. Nonetheless, my freelance career has spanned interesting times for writers. The massive expansion of newspapers and magazines in the late 1980s and early 1990s made a freelance career like mine possible, as did the swift improvement of technology. When Mrs Thatcher died in 2013, I spontaneously rejoiced, and contemplated arranging a street party. Having announced something to this effect on social media, I was roundly admonished by a fellow writer, a man so voluble and right wing his wife has since left him and his children cross the road to avoid him. I should be ashamed of myself, he said. Without Mrs Thatcher and her economic reforms, my career would have been impossible. I wasn't worthy to lick her boots. I should be worshipping at her shrine, yadda yadda yadda. I blocked him and got on with putting up the flags and bunting.

I actually think that my career wouldn't have been possible without the Apple Macintosh. I am not a bad writer, but I am a practised rewriter. Desktop and laptop computers, on which you can hone your prose until it squeaks, enabled me to make a living. I once tried to write on a typewriter, and I couldn't do it. Sentences do not form spontaneously in my mind. Not even that one did. Also, writing on a typewriter gave me appalling finger-ache. The muscles in my fingers, if there are any, weren't strong enough to take such a battering. Old-style journalists must have had fingers that positively bulged.

The golden years of journalism couldn't last and, of course, they didn't. In the past few years the internet has dealt a mortal blow to print. It's much harder now to conduct a successful career as a writer for magazines and newspapers than it used to be. The money isn't there, and most of the jobs are being done in-house by seventeen-year-old interns who think a semi-colon is a type of rodent. Many writers of my acquaintance have, in the customary euphemism, 'left the industry'. Some are now teaching journalism, while one or two may have starved to death. I have a regular pub lunch with a couple of writer friends, at which we all complain about money and pretend we are going back home afterwards to do some work, rather than have a nap. I asked them, how many actual full-time writers do you think there are in this country, i.e. people who make a living purely from their words? We were not counting anyone who has a real job, even if it's an editorial job, anyone who has family money, and anyone who has a rich spouse. This last qualification counted out one of the three of us, but it left the other two. We all thought for a few moments, and the highest number anyone came up with was two thousand. It was just a guess, but I think it's a high guess. Under a thousand would be more like it. Five hundred might be nearer the mark. Is two hundred too many?

(On further reflection we decided this was no bad thing. The fewer writers there are left, the more work there is for us. Writers aren't very nice people.)

This book, then, has two functions: to act as a personal memoir of an intriguing era, and to see whether much of my old stuff bears up. In the interest of fairness, I have put in several pieces that I know aren't much good. I suppose we need to show growth or improvement, partly because all writers are creatures of ego who think, probably wrongly, that the work they did yesterday was the best thing they have ever done. I have written a lot over the years about pop music, and it seems to me that pop musicians are always aware when their best years have been, because those are the songs that everyone wants to hear at live concerts. No wonder they all take drugs and kill themselves. Fancy having had one hit in 1978 and then having to play it every single night for the next fifty years.

Writers don't usually have to worry about their past. They never read their old work so they have no idea whether they have got worse or better. When people tell them what they think of their work, most of them have a filter system, built into the mighty stone ramparts of their well-defended egos: they hear praise, and listen to it, and own it; and they disregard all hostile criticism, although curiously they often remember the names of anyone who has been horrible to them in print, and vow to do them down eventually. I can still remember the name of the man who gave me my first bad review in 1980. I'll get him sooner or later, if he and I are still alive.

It is a strange life, and no mistake. We may look normal enough, and occasionally we even behave normally, but normal we are not. Virginia Woolf has a glorious passage in her novel *Orlando* about a character who is trying to write:

> Anyone moderately familiar with the rigours of composition will not need to be told the story in detail; how he wrote and it seemed good; read and it seemed vile; corrected and tore up; cut out; put in; was in ecstasy; in despair; had his good nights and bad mornings; snatched at ideas and lost them; saw his book plain before him and it vanished; acted his people's parts as he ate; mouthed them as he walked; now cried; now laughed; vacillated between this style and that; now preferred the heroic and pompous; next the plain and simple; now the vales of Tempe; then the fields of Kent or Cornwall; and could not decide whether he was the divinest genius or the greatest fool in the world.

Or both. Possibly at the same time.

1

Cheap Suit and Chirpy Demeanour

'The difference between stupidity and genius is that genius has its limits.'

Albert Einstein

I left university in the summer of 1981 with a double third in maths. How does a mathematician become a writer? With great difficulty, it turns out. I went along to the University Appointments Committee to discuss my career options. A man with an early suggestion of a combover sat behind a desk and gave me the lowdown. I could be an actuary, he said, or a statistician. Or I could become a maths teacher.

I want to be a comedy writer, I said.

A terrible weariness came into the poor man's eyes. He tried not to sigh, but couldn't stop himself.

Or I want to go into publishing, I said.

There were no jobs in publishing this year, even for English graduates, he said.

He was right about that. The only one I even applied for was a salesman's job in Nigeria. I'm quite pleased I didn't get that.

The only person I knew who did get a job in publishing was my friend Stuart, who was recommended to William Collins & Sons by his tutor. He said it was a bit like applying to MI5.

You could be an actuary, or a statistician, said the man again. Or you could become a maths teacher.

I quite fancy going into the BBC, I said. To produce programmes, I said.

Unfortunately, 1981 was right in the middle of a vast recession, with the worst job prospects for graduates in living memory. A year later, 30 per cent of graduates from my university would still be unemployed. I was one of them. I had moved back down to my mother's flat in north London, where I could be poor and miserable in relative comfort. In two and a half years, between June 1981 and January 1984, I applied for 154 jobs, most of them graduate traineeships in businesses I had no real interest in at all. Does anyone truly want to be a banker, or work in advertising, or management consultancy? I'm not sure I did but I was willing to give it a go. Unfortunately, I looked terribly young, for genetic reasons beyond my control. At twenty-one and twenty-two I could have passed for a more than averagely mature fourteen-year-old. Even more unfortunately, I *was* terribly young. University hadn't matured me despite all its best intentions, and the experience of being a not-very-good mathematician had fatally undermined my confidence. You may have heard of impostor syndrome, which many people, some at the peak of their careers, admit to suffering from. All of them are waiting for someone to tap them on the shoulder and say, 'You're no good at this, and we've just found you out.' I have never suffered from this because my failure was real. I was a perfectly good mathematician at school and did passably well in my A levels. But at university I was rumbled.

It took me many years to work this out, but eventually I realised that for all mathematicians south of Stephen Hawking, there's a glass ceiling that can never be broken, and that's the limit of your talent. For some people, it might be 2+2=4. For others it's calculus at O level or GCSE, and for me it was my end-of-first-year exams, paper 3, mechanics. Couldn't do it. Hadn't a clue about any of it. Wrote my name at the top of the paper and a couple of beginnings of answers and left the exam after an hour. Got six marks out of a possible two hundred. For anyone else to get a double third (third in first-year exams, third in final-year exams) would have been abject humiliation. For me it was a heroic triumph against the odds.

(Only in the past five years have I stopped having dreams in which I'm sitting a maths exam and I haven't a clue where to start. That's thirty years plus, more than a life sentence for murder.)

While interviewing me, potential employers could see through my cheap suit and unfeasibly chirpy demeanour to the fearful boy underneath, and decided to look elsewhere for their employees. I couldn't blame them. I wouldn't have employed me. In the context of my later career, though, the two and a half years of joblessness were a boon. With nothing much to do other than apply for jobs I wasn't going to get, I spent most of my time writing, writing, writing. Malcolm Gladwell was right. In order to become really good at something – whatever it is you want to do – you have to spend ten thousand hours practising. I was writing because I felt I had something to say, even if no one was ever going to read it. I actually wrote (and rewrote and rewrote) a complete book-length manuscript, called *The Bumper Book of Unemployment*, which I think had its moments. It was a comic extravaganza, fuelled by misery, and using all manner of satirical and comedic devices to approach its dismal subject. When it was finally done, I sent it to Stuart, my friend who was working in publishing. He said it showed promise but it wasn't for them. He'll go far, I thought. (He did.)

I'd love to read *The Bumper Book of Unemployment* again, but foolishly I threw it away years ago in a random fit of embarrassment. Foolishly, because all copy can be recycled sooner or later, as this book will prove.

Nonetheless, it did what it needed to, which was to help me find my voice as a writer and give me the confidence to use it. When I finally got a job, with my 155th application, for a PR company in central London, marketing Trivial Pursuit and Care Bears, I was a passable writer, although, as it turned out, a terrible PR man.

(I still have dreams in which I have run out of money and been compelled to take another job with this company, which in real life ceased to exist decades ago. They're very kind to me, but my continued inability to do the job is a source of pain and embarrassment to us all.)

All the time, I was writing, writing, writing, by myself and also in collaboration with my old friend and writing partner Harry Thompson. I'd known Harry since school and through university; we had written comic magazines and performed diabolically unfunny humorous revues together; and by 1985 he had acquired a wonderful job as a radio producer in BBC light entertainment. So we wrote a sitcom pilot called *Lenin of the Rovers*, which would star Alexei Sayle as Ricky Lenin, communist overlord of struggling football club Felchester Rovers. It was commissioned, and ran to two series of four episodes each, but the whole production was dogged by bad luck. Cast members kept disappearing into hospital for routine check-ups, and the next you heard, their funeral was on Tuesday. Then the Heysel stadium disaster happened and Radio 4's over-cautious executives immediately cancelled the second series, which had been recorded but not yet broadcast. The show is said to have attained cult status, which means that no one has ever heard of it, literally no one at all. I thought this minor success foretold a great comedy writing career for the two of us, and envisioned us receiving more Baftas than we could carry. Actually, that did happen to Harry, who went on to be producer of *Have I Got News For You* and later a best-selling biographer and novelist, before dying ridiculously young at the age of forty-five. We continued to write together for several years, but less and less effectively, with less and less success. I have had a CD of *Lenin of the Rovers* on the shelf next to my desk for about a decade. One day I might listen to it.

By autumn 1986 the second series of *Lenin* had been pulled, Harry and I had written and published four very short, silly loo books which, again, no one had noticed, and I was jobless again. Every failure feels like the last failure, before you have to go and work in B&Q. In the nick of time, though, I secured my second real job, as staff writer, and one of an editorial team of four, on a kids' computer magazine, *Your Sinclair*. Even for the time, the Sinclair 48K Spectrum was a pretty rudimentary piece of equipment, known to its fans as the electric beermat; but it was the computer most British kids owned, and many games were being written for it. Our magazine was *Smash Hits* for teenage computer geeks. It was great fun to write and very hard work. At *Your Sinclair* I learned to write fast on a 512K Apple Macintosh computer, then at the absolute forefront of nerd cool. It was invaluable training, although as previously mentioned, the boozing was excessive. I used to lie on the office floor from time to time with appalling stomach cramps, which should have been a warning. I was probably lucky to get out of there alive.

What are we like at twenty-six? I myself was driven, frightened and oddly incautious. I fell in love with some girl or other almost every day, and I doubt any of them even guessed. And in the evenings and weekends, when by rights I should have been lying in a darkened room to recover from the horrors of the week, I somehow found the energy to try to launch a freelance career, by writing things on spec and sending them off to people who didn't want to read them. And this was where I had my first stroke of exceptional good luck.

I had been reading the *Spectator* for some years, mainly because in those days I was quite a small-c conservative sort of boy, and I found its splenetic disapproval of the modern world rather to my taste. I had noticed that, over the course of a year, the magazine had published three pieces about pop music. Each had been by a different writer, and each was terrible. The magazine was obviously looking for someone to do this job on a regular basis, and I thought, why not me? So I wrote three sample columns and sent them in. With the naïveté of youth, and no idea of how the world worked, I thought someone might read them, recognise my talent and give me a column.

At most magazines the unsolicited manuscripts sit in a cardboard box in a corner, before finding their way into a black bin liner and out of the back door. If you are lucky, they send you a rejection slip. I was luckier. The editor's secretary, Jenny Naipaul, had injured her back and was in hospital in traction, bored to distraction. She offered to read the unsolicited manuscripts to fill the yawning hours. Most were as bad as she had expected, but she read mine and liked them. When she left hospital and returned to work, she rang me up and invited me in to see her new boss, Charles Moore.

In those days the *Spectator* occupied an elegant Georgian town house in Doughty Street, Bloomsbury, which I believe it owned outright. Its legendary summer parties were held within its rooms and in its modest back garden, where the great and good of London political, literary and journalistic life drank free gin until there was none left, anywhere in the world. Now I was sitting on the sofa in Charles Moore's office on the first floor at the front of the building, a room full of books, paintings, old furniture and teetering piles of paper, the study of all our dreams. Behind the desk sat Charles himself, barely three years older than me, and wearing the brightest red corduroys I had ever seen. If a pair of trousers can ever be said to be intimidating, these could. I tried not to stare. Charles, meanwhile, was effortlessly courteous and encouraging, and by the end of the meeting I had been commissioned to write something on the tenth anniversary of punk, on which Charles was possibly not an expert. But then I wasn't either. All I really knew of the subject was that I knew very slightly more than he did.

(Many years later I edited a book for the *Spectator* and told this story in the introduction. Charles read it and sent me an email. He said he'd never owned a pair of bright red corduroys and couldn't imagine what I thought I'd seen. I don't doubt him, but I'm sure he was wearing them. Was my imagination working overtime? Had he had an accident with his real trousers and was wearing the spare pair of bright red corduroys that every sensible office keeps for emergencies? Or had his later eminence, as editor of the *Daily Telegraph* and biographer of Mrs Thatcher, blanked out all memories of such frivolous vestments?*)

I wrote the punk piece, which went in the magazine, and I looked forward to the offers that would now come my way. National newspapers? Books? Screenplays? In my head I was already composing the text for the lucrative lecture tour that would surely follow before I realised that, actually, nothing had happened at all. I had had a piece in a magazine. The world had glanced at it and turned over to read Jeffrey Bernard.

And then I had my second stroke of good fortune.

Jenny Naipaul had been the editor's secretary for a number of years, and in the spring of 1987 Charles Moore promoted her to arts editor. One of the first things she did was call me up and offer me a regular monthly column on pop music. I almost bit the phone in half. How many words? What was the fee? What's the deadline? (The three questions a freelance learns to ask without even thinking.) The fee was abject, but I was well enough brought

* I recently asked Jenny Naipaul about the red corduroys. She said she couldn't really remember them, but then she couldn't not remember them either. They might have been, they might not have been. They were, in short, Schrödinger's Trousers.

up not to show my disappointment. And so I began my stint as the *Spectator*'s pop music critic. There were a few harrumphs of dismay on the letters page. Most *Spectator* readers were ageing, rubicund men who knew only one thing about pop music, which was that they didn't like it. It was an appointment of almost surreal absurdity, like being the cricket correspondent of the *NME*.

Here's an excerpt from the first column I still have a copy of, dated 17 October 1987. The previous half-dozen have gone missing, presumably because they were even worse than this:

> Up to the minute as always, I have just bought my first Walkman, a mere six or seven years after everyone else. Taking it on holiday to the Dordogne, I was disappointed by its lack of flexibility as a means of listening to music. No longer was it possible merely to bung on a record and do something else at the same time. No longer could I ignore the album's weaker tracks. And worse of all, no longer was it feasible to sing along in the reedy Berkmann tenor, as the tuneless caterwauling thus produced (you can't hear your own voice) managed to offend everyone within earshot, and sometimes substantially further.
>
> But I suppose we shall have to get used to the things. Cassette sales last year overtook albums for the first time, Walkmans being partially to blame. I myself have one of the latest hi-tech multi-coloured ones with millions of knobs and dials and headphones that extend right into the ear's inner recesses, presumably so that no one nearby is disturbed. It's all nonsense, of course. Besides the worrying possibility of the speakers snapping off, which would necessitate major surgery, everyone can still hear every note. Perhaps we should accept that train journeys will forever be rendered intolerable by the toosh-whack-tooshwhack emanating from the glassy-eyed idiot to your right.

Though just twenty-seven, I have already successfully assimilated the pompous, verbose and middle-aged tone of the magazine. Consciously or unconsciously? I don't know. But whatever was going on inside my head, I was writing about young people's music as a paid-up young person pretending to be an old person for money. It wasn't even very much money. And yet everything, my entire career, emanates from this one column. It seems extraordinary now. It seemed extraordinary then.

After my intemperate attack a couple of months ago on the mere notion of seeing the Rolling Stones on their current Hand Over All Your Cash This Minute tour (or whatever it's called), it was perhaps inevitable that I should end up witnessing their very first date, a fortnight or so ago in downtown Rotterdam ...

It seems to me odd and not a little sad that, after thirty years, pop music has finally come down to this. By any normal criteria, the Stones are completely past it. It's years since they produced a record of lasting quality, and even longer since they had anything remotely resembling a new idea. And yet, as well as enjoying the respect generally accorded to the irrevocably clapped out, they remain the world's most popular live band and, on the basis of this tour at least, easily the richest.

To maximise earnings, though, one does have to play the sort of places that one might never wish to visit personally. Rotterdam, a conglomeration of chemical works conveniently intersected by motorways, makes Birmingham look like Venice, and Feyenoord Stadium is scarcely one of international football's more glamorous venues. But the Rolling Stones were there, and so were the rest of us, jumping up and down on our plastic moulded seats and spilling Oranjeboom all over each other ...

As always at outdoor concerts, the sound appeared
to have been filtered through a sixty-foot woollen sock,
and you needed the Hubble telescope to see the stage.
Naturally none of this bothered the Dutch, whose wispy
beards vibrated as one to the music ... All the hits were
played, starting, not surprisingly, with 'Start Me Up',
and moving on even more appropriately with 'Sad Sad
Sad'. The set appeared to be constructed out of yellow
corrugated iron, presumably to give it a 'street' feel, even
if none of the individual band members have actually
walked down a street for twenty-five years. Mick Jagger
started with a red guitar, but soon changed to a blue one,
for no doubt pressing artistic reasons.

9 June 1990

If anything powered the column, it was a long-standing irrita-
tion with almost all writing about pop music. I had been reading
the *NME* religiously for a dozen years, but I hated its reverence for
the pop music canon, which admired old bores like Neil Young and
worshipped the Velvet Underground above all else. I also had an
inconvenient taste in music. I loved clever, complex acts like 10cc,
Steely Dan and XTC. I could see no point in Bruce Springsteen.
And I detested the Velvet Underground, although I did have a copy
of Lou Reed's later solo album *Transformer*, produced by David
Bowie and full of good tunes. If you were talking to proper rock
critics and admitted to this, they would probably spit on you. So
actually the *Spectator* was rather a good home for me.

In these recessionary times, it's oddly satisfying to
note that even the pop industry, once universally recognised as the last bastion of mindless extravagance, has
finally started to address the problem of overmanning.
Kraftwerk, for many years made up of four grim Germans

pretending to be robots, are now just two grim Germans pretending to be robots. The other two have been fired* and, if the group's recent videos are anything to go by, replaced by real robots.

But perhaps surprisingly, it's the Liverpudlian group Orchestral Manoeuvres in the Dark who have set the finest example. Once a thriving four-piece, they have recently become a thriving one-piece, named Andy McCluskey. Not that Mr McCluskey seems keen to publicise this unusual development: on his/their new album *Sugar Tax* (Virgin) no mention of the group's personnel (or lack of them) is made at all. Instead he now appears to use the name 'Orchestral Manoeuvres in the Dark' as his own personal pseudonym, an arrangement that no doubt boosts record sales, although it may cause the odd problem in restaurants.

13 July 1991

Every summer the *Spectator* hosts a giant and very boozy party in its offices and back garden. In Doughty Street, where the garden was long and thin and as crowded as a subway train in the Tokyo rush hour, the party was as much a physical challenge as anything. Reaching the end of the garden might take half an hour, and you might find nothing there other than a few cartoonists passed out under a bush. I learned many things from *Spectator* parties. One is to eat something beforehand. There is no food and there is unlimited drink. One year they were serving stiff gin and tonics to everyone, and when I left I was walking innocently down the street when, without any provocation whatsoever, the pavement suddenly rose up and assaulted me about the head. It was the first and, I'm happy to say, last three-day hangover I have ever suffered.

---

* They hadn't. They had left of their own accord. Fortunately their lawyers didn't read this.

The party always kicks off at 6.30 and these days I invest in either a late pub lunch, or possibly an early dinner, at 4.30.

I have met all sorts of famous people at *Spectator* parties. A Booker Prize-winner once chatted me up for nearly an hour, I now realise, for it wasn't until fifteen years later that I discovered he was gay. I spoke to Hilary Mantel a few times when she was the magazine's film critic, and we used to complain about how badly we were paid. I met Boris Johnson two or three times when he was editor. Then, seven years later, at a *Spectator* party, I walked up to him and he said 'Hello, Marcus', as though we had last talked seven minutes ago, not years. You can't help but be impressed by this, although his roving eye was legendary. If a reasonable-looking young woman walked in the room, he was off like a velociraptor.

> Is it really tough at the top? Furious debate on the subject continues to rage in rock circles following Phil Collins' savage denunciation of Eric Clapton in last month's *Q* magazine. 'How can he stand up there in a £5,000 suit and play the blues?' asked Phil, and the world nodded its head sagely and asked, 'Yes, how can he?' By charging £22.50 a ticket for a dozen gigs a year at the Albert Hall, that's how, but of course poor Eric took the question seriously, and in a long and heartfelt interview tried to justify his existence. 'The point is ... that blues is a state of mind, it's got nothing to do with acquisition. I can have all the money and cars in the world and still be very unhappy.' Tears welled from my eyes as I read these almost unbearably moving words.
>
> *5 March 1994*

How did I survive? I have often wondered. With hindsight I think there were two significant factors: I kept my head down;

and sheer dumb luck. Several people have since told me that they would have loved to have that column themselves, the implication being that they could have done it better, but they never told the editor of the time that. I survived six editors in the end. One or two of them simply couldn't care less. One editor cared too much, but he didn't last long enough to sack me. And then, suddenly, after twenty years or so, you're a fixture and they don't want the hassle of getting rid of you. Most editors like a quiet life. By simply doing nothing, they find that nothing has to be done. I can understand that position entirely.

> Under the Christmas tree lurks a package with your name on it. It is, you estimate, five and a half inches long, five inches wide and about a third of an inch thick. It rattles when shaken. It is unequivocally a compact disc. But is it a compact disc you would be happy to own? Or is it the new one by Phil Collins?
>
> It's a familiar tale. This year, as every year, thoughtless relatives are rampaging through record stores looking for something they have heard of, on the curious assumption that, if they have heard of it, you are going to like it. Mr Collins does not release his albums a month before Christmas for nothing. Obviously, no one is going to buy them intentionally, but you'd be amazed how many units you can shift in December by mistake.
>
> *14/21 December 1996*

Certain themes emerge from the column. Old rock stars are funny, and even when you think you have made every joke possible about Mick Jagger having a face like W. H. Auden's, another one is always just round the corner. Music itself is devilishly hard to write about, so let's avoid that if at all possible. Underlying it all, curiously, is a sort of fear, of trying desperately to keep up with musical trends, even though that ship sailed a while ago. For I started writing this column at the precise moment when I started to lose touch with youth culture. I never understood rap or acid house; I didn't like grunge; Oasis disgusted me viscerally. I was playing catch-up when I started, and yet somehow I hung on for more than twenty-five years.

This may seem like a humblebrag, but it isn't. I genuinely had little confidence in what I was writing. The excerpts here aren't bad, but a lot of the rest was terrible. Occasional bold flourishes of style could not compensate for an often terrifying shortage of content. For a long time I suspected that my *Spectator* column, which had been a huge help at the beginning, actually inhibited my wider journalistic career. Now I'm sure of it. You're never going to get into the *Guardian* writing that rubbish.

There were a couple of good ones, though, and this is one of them:

> It all started earlier this year, when my friend Chris managed to get four tickets for the first Leonard Cohen concerts at the O2. 'There's one for you if you want it,' he said. Well, obviously I wanted it, but cash was a little short at the time – in fact, not so much short as entirely absent, avoiding me as though I'd said the wrong thing. And I do have an ongoing tinnitus problem, the result of reviewing too many awful Tin Machine gigs for a certain crazed mass-market newspaper in the early 1990s.[*] Earlier this year I went to a friend's book launch held in a seedy West End dive where they played chart tunes at ear-splitting volume, and for a week afterwards I thought my head was going to explode. So I said no to Chris, with the greatest reluctance, and slight relief in the knowledge

---

[*]   You'll hear all about this in the next chapter.

that the £67 I didn't have, I still didn't have, rather than having £67 less than that.

But the Leonard Cohen concerts, as everyone will tell you, were life-changing events, not least for Leonard himself, whose money problems outclass my own in every way. A few weeks later Chris rang up again. 'I've got four more tickets for 13 November. There's one for you if you want it. And it really wasn't that loud. The sound quality is so good it doesn't have to be loud. Go on, you'll regret it if you don't.'

So, obviously, several months later I find myself on the Thames Clipper, surrounded by slightly worn-looking middle-aged people all buzzing with anticipation, or coffee. Laughing Len attracts a pangenerational audience – young people accompanying aged parents, with the occasional grandparent hobbling along behind, who bought Len's first album in 1967, or might have slept with him. There's also a glorious preponderance of attractive young Jewish women milling about but, overall, this is the crumbliest and most bourgeois audience for a gig I have ever seen.

The O2 itself is strangely reminiscent of Stansted Airport. Do you do your shopping before or after you go through security? One of our number had the lid of her bottle of water taken away by a Customer Safety representative, as the bouncers are now called. With its lid, apparently, the bottle could be used as a missile. Not that many of this audience could throw anything more than three feet ...

The stage, of course, is miles away. The musicians look like Oompa Loompas. Len himself looks gaunt and tiny, with a natty hat. 'Thank you for climbing these dizzy financial and architectural heights to get to your seats.

It's much appreciated. Thank you.' This will be the single most courteous gig I have ever attended. And Chris was right: the sound quality is astonishing and the volume is bearable, even for my ruined ears …

It seems extraordinary that these shows are only happening because Cohen's manager ran off with all his money. Was it a blessing in disguise? How must it be to feel all that love? It seems like the natural culmination of a unique career, and we feel honoured to be there to witness it. On the boat back, we say what can't really be said, that these might be his last concerts, without saying what is even more apparent: that this might have been the last one for a good proportion of the audience too.

6 December 2008

The end, when it came, was a surprise to everyone, including me. I had been editing a book called *The Spectator Book of Wit, Humour and Mischief,* which essentially involved sitting in Andrew Neil's office for a year, leafing through old binders. (He preferred the basement dining room, which was less out of the way.) As well as everything else, I read through my own columns and realised that having said something in 1992, I had said it again in 1995, 1999, 2003 and 2008. I was genuinely taken back by how little of my own stuff was good enough to go in the book. Everyone assumed this was modesty on my part, as opposed to shame. I tendered my resignation. In January 2016 my 346th and last column went in, more than twenty-eight years after the first. It was about David Bowie, as so often. Here's an excerpt from a better one, three years before:

I haven't heard the David Bowie album yet, but the Amazon order is in and Postie has been alerted as to the importance of the delivery. How often these days do any of us feel so excited about an imminent release? The ten-year gap between Bowie albums might have something to do with it, but the thirty-year gap between decent Bowie albums is probably more relevant. And all this is down to the excellence of the single. Gary Kemp of Spandau Ballet wept the first time he heard 'Where Are We Now?', and I was blubbing well into the song's third or fourth week on Radio 2.

Nostalgia for lost youth isn't exactly a new theme, but the song's grandeur and strange fragility seem to speak directly to the slightly melancholy middle-aged male, which is pretty much all of us. Convention would demand that after the second chorus you would get a third, which would edge the song perilously close to anthem territory. But, no, we cut straight to the coda, so after a long, slow build-up and a peak that is over before you know it, the song actually seems to end too quickly. Anyone who sees a parallel with life itself may already have celebrated their fiftieth birthday.

9 March 2013

2

Blood Trickling Out of Ears

'Writing is a trade ... which is learned by writing.'

Simone de Beauvoir

A question I am often asked, that every writer is asked all the time, is this: How do I get into the business? How do I get to do what you do?

Most writers haven't a clue how to answer this.

Everyone has a different story to tell. Some, like me, have one or two wondrous but unrepeatable strokes of luck that get them going. Others work their way up through the ranks the hard way, becoming reporters on local newspapers and wearing trilby hats with the word 'PRESS' written on a piece of card stuck in the hatband. Quite a lot of writers, it seems to me, have parents who are writers, who can introduce their hallowed offspring to newspaper editors at dinner parties, the mere thought of which gives me a pain all the way down my left side. Many putative writers are rich. They can hack it through the unpaid internships and the low-paid gofer jobs, because they know where their next meal is coming from, and their next three thousand meals. That gives me a pain all the way down my right side. This is why the staffs of most British newspapers, even the *Sun*, are dominated by public-school-educated poshos, while the clever sons and daughters of paups and immigrants become doctors and accountants.

In the interests of absolute clarity, I should probably say here that I went to a minor public school and Oxford, and that my father, in his relative youth, used to write wine columns for the *Daily Mail*. I'm sure that I benefited from the former, being able to talk the talk with *Spectator* editors wearing, or not wearing, memorable trousers. Did the latter help? My father would say definitely, but he is a lying, self-aggrandising sod who takes the credit for everything that isn't nailed to the floor. Also, we haven't spoken since 1975, for reasons I shan't go into here. My guess is that, in true Fleet Street tradition, my surname was a good calling card, but I wouldn't have got anywhere without a vestige of talent.

Let us therefore scroll back to early 1988, and a bench outside the Marquess of Granby pub in Rathbone Place, London W1. I am sitting with Sue Douglas, soon to take up a new job as features editor of the *Daily Mail*. She has read my first half-dozen pop columns in the *Spectator* and she has decided that I am the coming thing. I am probably grinning inanely. This is really all it takes to launch a thirty-year writing career, although I obviously do not realise that at the time. She says I should be patient, as it will all take a few weeks to sort out, and sure enough I am eventually offered a full-page column once a month to rant on about pop music. For this I will receive £250, which compares favourably to £80 a column at the *Spectator*, and roughly £8,000 a year for my full-time job at *Your Sinclair*. I am living in my mother's flat and I have no overheads. I go out and buy a stripy umbrella.

In these days before email, before even a fax machine had crossed my consciousness, you printed out your copy on paper and delivered it by hand. From my office to the *Spectator*'s was a twenty-minute walk, and a fifteen-minute walk back, because I was so relieved my copy had been accepted I walked much more quickly. The *Daily Mail* was different. I had to deliver my copy on a Thursday lunchtime for Monday's paper, which necessitated going to the *Mail*'s offices just off Fleet Street. Liveried doormen with a faint air of criminality prowled around downstairs and eventually let me in after my bona fides had been verified. The editorial floor upstairs was surrounded by vast quantities of dark-wood panelling and full of ancient wooden desks, many of them occupied by ancient wooden journalists. Sue Douglas had a largish office off to one side, an oasis of calm amid the hurly-burly and drunken growls of the main floor. She was a youthful and cheerful presence in an office characterised mainly by uncurtailed male aggression and ill-fitting suits. But she wouldn't be my main boss. That was another young woman called Corinna Honan, a year or two older than me, who had just been made showbiz editor and shared a rather smaller office, with a window out onto the floor, with her deputy, a massive old wreck called Bob, with a drinker's nose and a face as large as a hippo's. He also made strange little noises, apparently at random, as though snoring while awake.*

Once a month, then, in my lunch hour, I had to present my copy to Corinna and Bob, sit there while they read it, and hope beyond hope that they liked it. If they did, I could escape. If they didn't, I had to rewrite it then and there, with a pen. On rare occasions they didn't like it at all, and I had to go away, do a serious rewrite and redeliver the following day. Sometimes they were busy and didn't have time to read my copy immediately, and I had to sit there, waiting, as my lunch hour ticked away. Occasionally, as a distraction, Bob would scratch his armpit, and wait for retirement.

In circumstances like these, you learn quickly. You learn that

---

* Occasionally I'd go into the office later in the day, after Bob had had his liquid lunch. Then he would be snoring for real.

the verbose and middle-aged style favoured by the *Spectator* will not do. You learn that short words are better than long words, that short sentences are better than long sentences, and that long paragraphs will all be cut up into lots of shorter paragraphs. You learn quickly, to survive.

As it turned out, I didn't have a problem with the writing, but the social interaction was hellish. It would be difficult to overestimate how intimidating that editorial floor was, especially to someone as callow and weedy as I was. Corinna, hoping to round out my journalistic education, called me in to a couple of editorial meetings with the rest of the showbiz hacks, who hated my guts. I couldn't blame them. I had leapfrogged them all to a monthly column, and never had to do what they had all been doing for years, going out and finding stories in the old-fashioned way. One of them, an evil bastard with bright blue eyes, stared at me throughout as though he was going to beat me up if I tried to go to the loo. My utter inability to contribute anything to these meetings was quickly noted, and happily I was soon spared them. But the psychological wounds took some time to heal.

The *Daily Mail*'s house style hasn't changed much over the years. It smooths over the hard bumps in your copy, simplifies your more abstruse metaphors and takes out errant polysyllables (like 'errant' and 'polysyllable'). Having previously been rather precious about my copy, I learned not to be. As long as I was not utterly humiliated by the changes, and as long as I was paid, I kept my mouth shut. The hierarchy at the *Mail* is inviolable and based securely on fear, so the person who is changing your copy is only doing what they have been told to do and doing it to the best of their ability. You can throw the hugest tantrum in the world and you will change nothing, other than make the person in front of you hate you forever. You need to be *extremely* confident to lose your rag on a regular basis, although it has since occurred to me that it is the people like that who so often rise to the top, not worrying about the enemies they make on the way. How lucky to be so foolish.

Fortunately, I soon realised that Corinna was a useful ally. Not only was she young, she was a woman, and there weren't many of them around. The showbiz hacks hated her nearly as much as they hated me, but she was their boss, so they couldn't show it as often or with as much violence as they would have liked. Watching her dealing with their smelly-arsed sexism encouraged me in my own quieter struggle. I also got on well with the two gay members of the team: Jack Tinker, the tiny and flamboyantly camp theatre critic, and Lester Middlehurst, the only very slightly larger show-biz columnist. They were both kind and friendly to me whenever I met them, and god, did I appreciate it. Both dead now, of course. Neither of them reached sixty. Tabloid journalists rarely seem to live long lives.

By the early summer of 1988 I was getting more and more work from the *Mail*, I had discovered the joys of the fax machine, and the money I was earning from my freelance work in evenings and weekends far outweighed my feeble salary at *Your Sinclair*. The freelance life was beckoning me, the call of the wild. I resigned my job in June, and moved into the tiny flat I had bought in north London with a friend. Much change in a short time. I'm still free-lance, and I still live in the same flat, although now with a partner and two enormous children. Very little change in a long time.

By the autumn of 1988, as well as the pop column, I was writing pieces for Features and reviewing gigs overnight for Showbiz. They wanted the review in the paper the following morning for the same reasons that Jack Tinker always wrote his theatre reviews overnight: immediacy. But he'd leave the show when it was finished, take a cab to the office, type up his review and that would be it. My deadline was earlier and the gigs were usually later, so I had to leave most gigs after seven songs had been played, find a phone box and dictate my 350 words to a copytaker who rarely

knew how to spell 'Springsteen'.* This meant that I usually had to
write the first half of the review before the concert had begun. As
a result, the first half of the piece was usually quite good, while
the second half fell away a bit.

> If there is a word that sums up Julio Iglesias's performance
> last night, it is 'slithery'.
>
> Like a well-oiled piston, he slithered knowingly
> through his repertoire and sent his predominantly female
> audience wild with unabashed desire.
>
> Pop music has always been about sex, from Elvis
> onward. Today's young nubiles prefer, depending on
> age, the groomed alien perfection of Bros or the pelvis-
> thrusting hairiness of George Michael.
>
> But their older sisters, and possibly even brothers, buy
> Julio Iglesias albums. Julio knows this and his fondness
> for women is therefore well documented. For millions he
> is the personification of the holiday romance, the Waiter
> Incarnate.
>
> *24 November 1988*

All written while the support act was still playing.

When I had filed the review I usually went back to see the rest of
the concert, just in case the guitarist exploded. If Prince or Stevie
Wonder was playing, this was sheer pleasure. If it was Julio Iglesias
or, worst of all, Neil Diamond, it was torture. After a year or two of
this, I have to admit, I would leave the gig to phone in my copy and
then I would go home. The rush of adrenalin as I hopped on board
the tube train was usually the biggest thrill I had had all evening.

Many of these concerts were held at Wembley Arena, a huge
barn-like space in north-west London with legendarily poor sound.

---

* Francis Wheen remembers the weary air of old copytakers who would ask,
as one started dictating another paragraph, 'Is there much more of this?'

What the acoustics may have lacked in quality, though, they made up for in volume. If I was lucky I would be sitting right at the back, unable to see the performers, but able to hear them without blood trickling out of my ears. Once I had two tickets to see Bros, the weird pop twins who were the frequent butt of everybody's jokes, including mine. My friend Emma said she wanted to come too. We sat six rows from the front, and we were the tallest people there by about two feet. Everywhere, in all directions, were small girls screaming their hearts out. The band had to crank up the volume to Deep Purple levels if they were going to be heard at all. It was by miles the loudest concert I ever attended, and we lasted only the five or six songs I needed to write my review.

In February 1990 I went to see Bob Dylan at the Hammersmith Odeon:

> Bang on schedule, Dylan walked on stage and cranked into the first song. This was clearly one of those 'back-to-the-roots' affairs, with minimal lighting, the stage virtually empty of machinery, and the instrumentation of *Blonde on Blonde* vintage ...
>
> Uncommitted watchers, meanwhile, noticed the dire threat of the notorious harmonica, suspended menacingly under the great man's chin.
>
> After half a dozen songs – all of which, in true 'back-to-the-roots' style, sounded identical – he said, 'Thank you,' his first recorded words on stage since 1973. Then he smiled. The hippies behind me gasped with astonishment. But just as everything had been going so well, Dylan remembered his harmonica, and we were given the famous two-note solo, which he proceeded to repeat throughout the show.
>
> *6 February 1990*

In three years of reviewing gigs, I probably saw most of the big names at least once, but I swiftly learned that there is nothing less fun, simply nothing, than seeing a band live whom you don't like. You might get good copy out of it, and quite often I did, but after a while it begins to eat your soul for breakfast. One of the worst was Bruce Springsteen, who opened a British tour with an outdoor gig at Villa Park in Birmingham. Springsteen, as you may know, is a man of bristlingly authentic vision who believes strongly in value for money. In practice this means that he plays the same song over and over again for three and a half hours. I had an early deadline, so had to file after seven songs as usual, but all the hacks had been brought to the venue on a luxury coach, which would be taking us home again afterwards, so what could I do? I went back into the venue and reclaimed my seat, but my eyes began to swim and my ears began to ache with boredom and despair. Then I had an inspiration. When I had left the ground to find a phone box, I had noticed a tiny municipal garden just over the road. It had trees, it had flowers but most importantly it had a bench. The two hours I spent reading my book on that bench, vaguely listening out for exploding guitarists, were two of the happiest hours of my life.

The end came after a Tina Turner gig in Antwerp. The music wasn't so bad, but the volume was horrendous, and I had worryingly loud tinnitus for ten days afterwards. It subsided thereafter, but by then I had asked the showbiz desk to spare me any more live gig reviewing. Health reasons! Why hadn't I thought of that before? That was twenty-seven years ago, and I don't think I have been to more than half a dozen gigs since.

3

A Tincture or Twelve

'A lot of the time writing is completely tedious, but one good sentence can pay off for many, many years of hell.'

Kate Atkinson

The years 1988 to 1990 were, for me, hectic and exciting. The *Spectator* had led to the *Daily Mail*, and being all over the *Daily Mail* led to many other things. I was summoned to the offices of *You*, the *Mail on Sunday* magazine, to meet their tiny, furious editor Nick Gordon, a former *Daily Mail* executive who ruled his office like a fun-size Stalin. He offered me a contract – the first person to do that – for six pieces at £750 each, which was an extraordinary amount of money then, and would be now if you could ever get it, which you can't. This was a rather painful interlude in my life, for Nick and I discovered, at roughly the same time, what I could do and what I couldn't do. Reportage was fine as long as I didn't have to talk to anyone. Interviews were utterly beyond me. I flew to Milan for an hour with Mick Hucknall, asked him all the wrong questions – I asked him about the music rather than about his sex life – and saw a thousand-word piece reduced to a two-hundred-word picture caption. In a year I think I only wrote one piece that Nick really liked, which was a satirical takedown of some teenage girls who were fans of the band Bros, or 'Brosettes' as they liked to call themselves. I would soon learn that as a satirist you're always better advised to kick up than kick down, but even at the time I was uncomfortable with this, one of the few pieces I have written that I am genuinely ashamed of.* Nick Gordon soon stopped returning my calls and when my contract came to an end no one actually said anything, because no one had to say anything. The failure was too apparent.

Nonetheless, by going into that office several times, I met the magazine's staff and made some friends. (It's the one piece of advice I would give to young writers just starting out. Go and see people. Meet them face to face. It'll actually make it far harder for them to fire you later on when it all goes pear-shaped.) One such was David Thomas, an excitable Old Etonian in his early thirties with the temperament of a Labrador puppy. I have never known anyone with a faster mind than David, or a shorter attention span. He can write really good copy at extraordinary speed, and he's forgotten all about it a couple of hours later because he's doing something else. Towards the end of my *You* nightmare he left to become editor of *Punch*, the weekly humour magazine that hadn't been funny for decades. I had been a regular reader in the early 1970s but had been worn down by its complacency and clubbish-ness. Now in its dotage, it had become the magazine equivalent of passing the port to the left. David had the energy and the opti-mism to take on the job, and did the only thing he could do in the circumstances: he sacked almost all the contributors who hadn't already walked out in high dudgeon and started again from scratch.

---

* Some years later I was in Leicester Square tube when one of the former Brosettes recognised me. 'Shame on you!' she shouted, and she was right.

This process, happily, included me. I wrote a few features, which weren't bad, and in the summer of 1990 David offered me a fortnightly sports column, alternating with the eminent and hugely well-informed Patrick Collins of the *Mail on Sunday*. Although my knowledge of sport was meagre, my enthusiasm was boundless. Here's the beginning of the third column I wrote:

The technical side of golf tends to leave me a mite bamboozled. Although I can tell the difference between a good swing and a bad swing – Is he holding the club the right way up? Has he hit the ball? Has it gone more than three feet? – the finer points often elude me. Certainly I would have problems identifying the flaws, if any, in the swings of the top professionals, and sadly the commentaries of the experts – 'I think he blanted that one a touch there; perhaps he chopped a wee bit in his through-bundle' – leave me none the wiser.

All of which has made the acres of newsprint expended on Nick Faldo's 'drastically remodelled swing' in the weeks since his Open success all the more infuriating. Indeed, during the competition itself, the television commentators referred to the swing and its drastic remodelling even more than they referred to Payne Stewart's retina-damaging plus fours.

Nevertheless, it seems beyond all doubt that Faldo's new swing is the reason for his current world-beating form and we must take the experts' word. Or must we? After reading a spread in the *Daily Mail* – the inevitable 'Nick Faldo Story', featuring lots of embarrassing photographs of the lanky suburbanite aged fifteen – I have begun to wonder.

The photos that showed Faldo in the days before he won majors by five strokes were noticeably different from the photos of him since. The swing, the sweaters, the bland smiles: all looked much the same. But what had changed was his hair. At some point in the past five years, Faldo has had what Martin Amis would call a major rug rethink. Could this be the answer? Could it be that Faldo's success is due to a drastically remodelled haircut?

17 August 1990

Not too good, is it? Actually it was an embarrassment to type it in. Patrick Collins could bring broad sporting knowledge and deep insights to his contributions. I brought jokes about sweaters, plus fours and haircuts. One day George Best turned up on *Wogan*, having clearly been mopping up the stuff:

His main argument, that the BBC didn't deserve him sober for a mere £150, may not seem to hold much water, but then neither did George, it being not exactly one of his favourite liquids ...

It's in the lower echelons of sporting life, though, that alcohol really makes its presence felt. As a sportsman of modest skills myself, I have frequently taken recourse to the glug at moments of athletic stress, and have found the results most satisfactory.

Snooker, for instance, is not a game to be played sober unless, by some bizarre accident of fate, you are very good at it. If, like me, you play the sort of games of snooker in which two-thirds of the points scored can be attributed to unforced fouls, a tincture or twelve can help you effect the most surprising trick shots, such as the one where the cue ball hits the ball you're aiming at straight into the pocket.

19 October 1990

There's something there, a certain youthful *joie de vivre*, if we're being generous. But it's all too wordy and pompous, and constantly straining for effect. Even the author photograph that adorns the piece is so smug you want to hit it with a frying pan.

I reread these pieces for this book in a state of mystification and increasing horror. Why didn't they work? And why had I never realised they didn't work before?

Looking for an answer, I bought a few volumes of *Pick of Punch* from my local second-hand bookshop. Those from the 1970s featured some terrific cartoons and lots of unfunny pieces by people who should have known better. Keith Waterhouse, a fine columnist for the *Daily Mirror* and the *Daily Mail*, was terrible in *Punch*. Alan Coren, so droll on the *News Quiz* and in *The Times* in later years, raised scarcely a titter in his *Punch* pieces, and these were supposed to be his best of the year. Even Miles Kington, a hero of mine, was quashed by the mighty dullness of 1970s *Punch*, his jokes forcibly extracted from him, possibly without anaesthetic.

The later volume, edited by David, was even worse.

With hindsight I feel rather sorry for David and his team. They had energy, youth and talent – almost all of them went on to better things – but they were battling against insuperable odds. Most successful humorous magazines, like *Private Eye*, *Viz* and *Smash Hits*, are solidly non-conformist, even anarchic. They cock a snook at everything that deserves it. But *Punch*, even in its heyday, which I'm not sure ever existed, was male, conservative and a bit stuffy. In the early 1990s none of these were feasible options, and all that was left was the desperate need to be funny. But the magazine was never as funny as it thought it was, and not a fraction as funny as it needed to be.

Eventually it dawned on United Newspapers, who also the owned the *Daily* and *Sunday Express*, that the magazine was a waste of time, money and space. They pulled the plug in early 1992, and I lost three hundred quid a fortnight and maybe fifteen devoted readers. I admired those readers for their fortitude and tenacity, but they must be long dead by now, if they weren't long dead at the time.

4

Knockabout Laughs

'I wouldn't advise anyone who wants to be liked to write for a living.'

Suzanne Moore

In the spring of 1990, the *Daily Mail*'s legendary editor David English invited me in to lunch and asked me to be the paper's deputy TV critic. I had written the odd TV review since the previous autumn, but the official deputy was now retiring and his job was mine if I wanted it. I did want it, and English knew I wanted it. He was a real character, an absolute charmer, a sly, manipulative old bastard who ruled the paper like a medieval pope. Having greeted me in his enormous office, he could easily have taken me out of the building through the front entrance, which would have been discreet and very much easier for me (speaking as a person of introverted tendencies). But he deliberately led me through the huge open-plan editorial office to the lifts at the back of the building, to show everyone that I was, at that moment, the Favoured

One. The hacks looked at me with one of two expressions, undying hatred or obvious calculation. The latter group would be the ones who rang me up with commissions over the next few weeks and months, because to commission the Favoured One would put you in good odour with the boss. This is how you maintain power in an organisation like Associated Newspapers: with a beaming smile and the crack of the invisible whip in your hand.

I would be deputising for a man called Peter Paterson, who had been the paper's industrial correspondent and the *Spectator*'s political editor, and was now passing his final productive years in the cosy byway of TV criticism. I met Peter on several occasions and he was never less than lovely to me – possibly because he'd usually had a few by then – but he never concealed that he had no interest in the job at all. I was young and energetic, just thirty, and I felt slightly offended by his extreme personal laziness, which I understand rather better now, as I edge inexorably towards the age he was then. There were six TV reviews a week, from Monday to Saturday. Peter did Monday to Thursday, I would get Fridays and every other Saturday, and another writer called Jeannette Kupfermann had the other Saturday. Best of all, when Peter went on holiday, as he did quite a lot, exhausted by his toils, I would stand in for him on Monday to Thursday and Jeannette would stand in for me on Fridays and Saturdays. In this slightly ad hoc way, I would end up writing a total of 457 television reviews in just over seven years. The fee for the first one was £200, and because I was too afraid to make a fuss, the fee for the last one was £200 too.

By golly I loved this job. I had been obsessed by television all my life. I had watched far too much of it since childhood, and was now watching far, far too much of it. All the TV critics I would meet were the same. Jaci Stephen, then of the *Evening Standard*, later of the *Mail*, watched terrible telly late at night when she couldn't sleep, which I theorised she couldn't because she had spent all day watching terrible telly as well. As we were young and slightly bonkers, we genuinely enjoyed the process, which usually involved going into a preview theatre at the BBC or Thames TV or London Weekend TV (the two London ITV franchises at the time) and watching the show on videotape on a big screen by yourself. There was an important distinction between previewers (who recommend programmes before they are shown) and reviewers (whose opinions arrive in print after broadcast). Both sets of writers saw the programmes in advance, but the previewers all went to one big weekly screening, while reviewers were treated with slightly more respect. (Previewers, though, got a better and wider selection of biscuits. They were always quite insistent on this matter.) I could choose what I wanted to watch and wanted to review. As long as I filed exactly 610 words by 3 p.m. on the afternoon before publication, no one complained.

Peter told me that, by contrast, he never watched any TV other than the programmes he had to write about. He just couldn't be arsed. But his sheer professionalism trumped my energy and enthusiasm, because no one complained about his reviews either. We were deemed to be a good combination: his gravitas for most of the week, and my knockabout laughs for the last two days. I was almost certainly the only person who didn't see it this way, but I knew well enough by now to keep my head down and get on with it. Mildness of temperament is a useful attribute for any freelance writer, and if you don't have it, faked mildness of temperament will do just as well.

Without anyone having really noticed, I rather suspect that LWT's latest American import, *Beauty and the Beast* (ITV), may be turning into a bit of a cult.

Already the company's phone lines are besieged by a self-appointed 'fan club' whenever an episode is not shown. And with the show having picked up twelve Emmy nominations in America, we could be staring down the barrel of a substantial hit.

Stranger things have happened, of course, although you'd have to go far to find a stranger thing than *Beauty and the Beast*. Catherine (Linda Hamilton) may be extremely attractive and a very sympathetic character, but let's face it, she's in love with a man in a lion suit. And not any old man in a lion suit, but a highly intelligent, intuitive man in a lion suit who speaks very quietly and knows Tennyson backwards. In other words, the man in a lion suit of every woman's dreams.

Naturally, there are a few snags in their relationship. As Catherine herself says over the credits, 'Although we cannot be together, we'll never ever be apart.' Well, we all know what that means, and indeed, certain anatomical niceties do prevent the affair from reaching its natural culmination. Doomed love is very romantic, and as the violins swoop and swirl, Catherine and Vincent stare tragically at each other on the roof of her apartment. But how did he get there? New York may be an odd place, but even a man in a lion suit would get noticed occasionally, if not thrown into the nearest available zoo.

11 November 1989

In each piece I would usually review two shows, one at relative length and one in brief. Sometimes I'd do just one show, and other times three or four. This latter could be dangerous as there were often not three or four new shows to review on any one evening. For this was the era of four television channels, BBC1, BBC2, ITV and Channel 4. (Satellite television had been launched in February 1989 but no one watched it.) There were repeats à gogo and often there was nothing new to watch at all. As a reviewer, though, you at least had the benefit of knowing that if you wrote about something on ITV, ten million or so people were bound to have seen it. How TV critics cope now, with thousands of channels and audiences for a single programme rarely touching three million, I can't imagine.

> Anyone, with a bit of imagination and a handy thesaurus, can start an Alan Whicker sentence. 'Here in Hong Kong, where the high-rise buildings match the high-rise lifestyles, where the mystique of the East is ... er ...' But only the great man himself can actually finish them.
>
> *3 March 1990*

Does it matter that ratings have fallen so low? Probably not to people who work in television, or even to those who watch it, but it has been a disaster for TV critics. It is, or it used to be, a different kind of job to most criticism. If you're reviewing films or plays or books, by and large you have seen or read the films or plays or books before any of your audience. You are providing a consumer service. Go and see this. Don't bother with that. This requires a lot of exposition, as you have to explain in some detail what the film/play/book is about.

TV critics, by contrast, are writing for two sorts of people, those who did see the programme last night, and those who didn't. Those who didn't might still be interested in whether the programme is worth watching, because there may well be another episode next week. But you can't bung in loads of exposition to fill your 610 words because those who did see the programme, your primary audience, already know it all. What you have to do instead is come up with ideas and observations that haven't already occurred to them. You don't have to be right – and heaven knows, I was wrong an awful lot of the time – but you can't be dull. I can only be grateful that Clive James in the *Observer* and Nancy Banks-Smith in the *Guardian*, between them, had effectively created the gag-packed TV review in the 1970s and 1980s. People like me, Jaci,

Lynne Truss in *The Times* and Victor Lewis-Smith in the *Evening Standard* were happy just to tread in their giant footsteps.

Talking of Clive James ...

> After an uncertain start, the 459th series of *Dallas* (BBC1) is rapidly turning into a cracker. The boredom of last year is long gone, and with Cliff Barnes now back in his old role as JR's nemesis, things are undoubtedly looking up.
>
> And yet rumours abound that the ageing soap's viewing figures have fallen as low as five million a week, a mere bagatelle compared to the bulging audiences for Mrs Mangel and Dot Cotton. Could viewers finally be tiring of the unlikely make-up, the random facelifts, the lunches that no one ever eats?
>
> Fortunately, some things never change, such as the dialogue. Last night's was a particularly classic episode, featuring three of the most popular Dallas lines of all time: (i) 'Who could be calling at this hour?' (ii) 'I needed some time to work out my feelings,' and (iii) 'I'm not sure of anything any more.' The use of language in Texas's premier city remains fascinatingly idiosyncratic. The word 'yes', for instance, is never used. In *Dallas* the opposite of 'no' is 'I'd like that'.
>
> *3 May 1990*

How often did I go into the office? Never, if I could help it. The *Mail* had moved out of its ancient, Dickensian offices off Fleet Street and into an incredibly flash open-plan corporate headquarters in the old Barkers building in Kensington. You couldn't help but be impressed. The dodgy doormen had been pensioned off and replaced by slender young women with clipboards; the atrium was larger than my house, and there were so many plants the air inside actually seemed fresher than outside. Technology saved me from having to go there more than three times a year. I worked at home on my lovely new Apple Macintosh, watched TV in the afternoon, wrote up the review the following morning and filed it at the last minute at the print shop up the road, where they had a fax machine and charged fifty pence a page. It was very nearly the perfect existence.

> *Island Son* (ITV) is the new Richard Chamberlain vehicle, and watching it is a salutary experience. Chamberlain, of course, is mainly famous for looking fresh-faced and eager in *Dr Kildare* a quarter of a century ago. Now he's Dr Daniel Coloni, based in Hawaii and, presumably thanks to expensive surgery, just as fresh-faced as ever. The texture of the Chamberlain skin is remarkable: it so shines with health you could probably comb your hair in it.
>
> *23 June 1990*

Every writer has his 'home' subjects, the things he is obsessed by, the ones that come round again and again. Mine turned out to be plastic surgery, men with beards, silly hairstyles, terrible dialogue and the horrible clothes people wore. At times, though, I could be as pompous as anyone else, usually when reviewing a documentary that I would never have bothered watching if there had been anything else to write about. As with my pieces in *Punch*, rereading these old reviews after all this time has been another salutary experience. At the time I thought I was doing the most important job in the world, but there's a saying you often hear from people who work in television: 'it's only telly'. I always thought this was people being incredibly cynical about what they were doing, and that they all really thought telly was the most important thing in the world. In fact, I still think that, but I also think that, in their strange and indirect way, they were telling the truth. It *was* only telly.

In *Stars In Their Eyes* (ITV), 'ordinary' (i.e. drastically untalented) people impersonate their favourite singing stars and compete for a place in the Grand Final. The winners so far have been a Shirley Bassey clone, a financial consultant who did Chris de Burgh, and a Chinese Tom Jones. But much the best performance in the show is undoubtedly that of the compère, who does an inspired impersonation of Leslie Crowther, vermilion hair and all. It's a skilful parody: the showbiz enunciation, the gushing sincerity ('Well bless her heart, wasn't that absolutely sensational?'), even Crowther's slightly embalmed look are perfectly reproduced.*

13 August 1990

Why did I never ask for a pay rise? God, that annoys me now. But for all my confidence on the page, I was terribly lacking in confidence in real life. Occasionally I would go into the office to have lunch with Sue Douglas and remind everyone else I was still alive and available for work. The entrance to the editorial floor, where maybe fifty people sat, was at one corner of a huge square, and her office, encased in glass, was at the diagonally opposite corner. The walk from one to the other lasted several hours and was at least three miles long. By the time I reached her office, I was dripping with sweat and could barely speak. I don't suffer from such crippling shyness any more, but I now recognise it as a disability that blighted my life for a number of years. My bank balance, too, it turns out.

It would be an outrageous calumny to suggest that the average British television viewer is primarily interested in smut, gossip and scandal to the exclusion of all else.

---

* The show was hosted by the real Leslie Crowther.

But how many people can have tuned into this week's *Hollywood Legends* (C4) programme on Rock Hudson without wondering when someone would mention ... you-know-what?

The programme was an almost total whitewash ... The clue to its intentions came in the title. 'Legend' is one of those words, like 'genius' and 'classic', that, after years of thoughtless abuse, have finally been rendered meaningless. Just as genius is now applied to the moderately talented, and classic merely means old, so legendary has become just another word for dead. Hudson certainly qualified on that score, but as the large number of clips of his films showed, he didn't just look like a giant redwood tree – he acted like one, too.

20 August 1990

I think we can probably stop there. Television criticism can become repetitive, as I have just learned by reading my own. But for seven years at the *Daily Mail* it was my daily bread. For a while I also had a Saturday column full of more general TV-related jokes, but to be frank it was more notable for the fee it generated (£500) than for its content. In the end, I wrote about TV for so long that I began to think of myself as a 'TV critic'. This meant raised levels of self-importance, accompanied by the ceaseless thwarted rage that Peter Paterson would not retire and give me his job. I wasted years fretting about this, because at that time of your life you genuinely believe that your career is the most important thing in the world. If you have got nowhere, you desperately want to get somewhere. If you have got somewhere, as I had, you desperately want to get somewhere else, preferably somewhere higher. You're in a race, but you don't know where the race is going, or how long it's going to last, or why you're in the race at all. You think that, to take an example completely at random, to become the main TV critic of the *Daily Mail* rather than the deputy TV critic is going to make a difference to your standing in the world. Men will raise an approving eyebrow, women will swoon into your waiting arms and editors will offer you work, just because you're you. It's just as well that ambition is a disease of the young, because otherwise we'd all go completely mad.

In truth, I did well to survive as long as I did. In 1992 David English retired from the editorship of the *Daily Mail* and was promoted to chairman. His successor was his former number two, Paul Dacre, a very different character. The whip in English's hand was usually invisible, but Dacre was more puritanical, less humorous and around a thousand times more terrifying. When he became editor, he took me for a get-to-know-you lunch at Claridge's. I was my usual jolly, faintly frivolous self, not knowing how badly this would go down with a man who may have been born with a deep frown line between his eyebrows. I wouldn't say we didn't get on, but we didn't bond like brothers, and in fact I never met him again. I continued to write TV reviews for another three and a half years, but towards the end of that time it was apparent that I was yesterday's man. When Sue Douglas was appointed editor of the *Sunday Express* in 1996, she asked me to be her TV critic and I jumped at the chance. That's another story, an even more depressing one as it happens. But I was right to go. Several years later Peter Paterson finally retired, and the *Mail* replaced him with . . . no one at all. Dacre decided that the job of TV critic wasn't required any more. Imagine if I had stayed, and that had happened. Imagine the humiliation.

5

Days of Plenty

'Only the privileged and the naive believe people's achievements are purely the product of their own genius.'

Gary Younge, Guardian

I met Ian Hislop in the first term of my second year at university. He was, as you might expect, a very funny man, although unlike many people who go on to write comedy for a living, he smiled and laughed a lot. (I used to know a comedy writer who'd say 'very funny', and mean it, without ever cracking a smirk.) Ian asked me to be in a revue he had written, which was the first mistake he made. It's useful to discover at the earliest possible moment your limitations as a performer, and mine was a complete lack of talent. Other revues of his went ahead without me, but the friendship remained as firm as ever. After we left university we used to hang around together, as he was trying to make his way at *Private Eye*, and doing some English tutoring in his spare time, and I was loitering without intent at home, wondering what on earth to do with my life. Ian always knew what he was going to do with his life, and he has done it. I have never known anyone so focused and ambitious, who nonetheless has lived his life with complete integrity. Some years ago, when he was still editor of the *Daily Mirror*, Piers Morgan took against Ian for some reason – possibly because he was always calling him 'Piers Moron' in the *Eye* – and had a couple of reporters investigate him, looking for dirt. They spent six months tailing him and looking through his bins, and they found nothing, because there was nothing to find.

Ian flourished at *Private Eye*, wrote for *Spitting Image* in its glory days with his schoolfriend Nick Newman, and, again with Nick, invented Tim Nice-But-Dim for Harry Enfield. Richard Ingrams made him his deputy editor, mainly because he recognised that Ian was equally good at the two disjointed parts that make the *Eye* what it is. He was, clearly, a gifted comic writer, and sat in with the main joke writers (Ingrams, Christopher Booker, Barry Fantoni) from an early stage. But Ian could also do the journalism, an entirely different skill. It's a rare enough combination that when Ian goes on holiday, he hands over editorial responsibility to Nick for the jokes and the actual deputy editor, Francis Wheen, for the journalism. They are both exceptional at what they do, but they couldn't do the other man's job in a million years.

In October 1986 I got a phone call from one of the receptionists at the *Eye* saying, drop everything, be at the Criterion bar at Piccadilly Circus at half past six. There were about eight or ten of us there, feeling slightly excited and suitably mystified, although like an idiot I said, as soon as Ian turned up, 'This had better be good.' It was good: at the age of twenty-six Ian had been appointed editor of *Private Eye*.

His first couple of years in the job were tough. Some of the old guard (Peter McKay, Nigel Dempster, Auberon Waugh) were appalled that this young shaver had been promoted above their fine, noble brows, and did everything they could to undermine him. At the same time, Richard Ingrams had run the magazine on a publish-and-be-damned basis, which often turned out to be publish-and-be-sued. He was a contrarian and an anarchist, who liked to make trouble just to see what would happen. Ian was and remains a more cautious man, but then you could hardly be less cautious than Richard. In this case, though, Richard had made a sound decision. With the assistance of two managing directors, Dave Cash until 2000 and Sheila Molnar ever since, Ian has turned the magazine into possibly the only journalistic outlet that everyone still trusts, as well as a consistently funny supplier of topical gags and cartoons. He has now been editing the magazine for more than half of his (and my) life.

I should probably add here that Ian is exactly one day older than me, and we both lost our fathers at a difficult age, Ian's to stomach cancer when he was thirteen and mine to the Polish au pair when I was fourteen. He has been a good and steadfast friend to me and I hope I have to him too. I am not going to pretend that being his friend has not been a useful boost to my career. But who becomes friends with people because you think they may be in a position to do you a few favours ten years down the line? There is luck in this, as there is in anything. When I mentioned this to Ian a few years ago, his slightly irritable response was 'I wouldn't have brought you into the magazine if you hadn't been any good.' Which is fair enough, and I believe him.

I wrote my first piece for the *Eye* in 1989. For a number of years I was, again, a deputy TV critic, writing vicious reviews of shitty programmes under the byline Old Couch Potato. The main critics were called Square Eyes and, later, Remote Controller, and their identities were known by only six people, including themselves and, oddly enough, me. Apparently they would be in breach of their contracts at various media organisations, and although (as far as I'm aware) they are no longer under contract to anyone, still almost no one knows who they are. It's possible someone did know and has long since forgotten.

> Hidden away in the wilderness of BBC2's Sunday after-
> noon schedules is yet another of Janet Street-Porter's
> exciting new 'yoof' programmes, the second revival of
> *Juke Box Jury*. (The first, presented a decade ago by resi-
> dent beardie Noel Edmonds, was swiftly airbrushed from
> corporation history.) So disastrous has this run been that a
> second series is widely expected in the new year.
>
> *10 November 1989*

I never bothered to hide my own identity, because I was con-tracted to nobody and I was proud of the work I did and wanted everyone to know about it. Oddly enough, I met Janet Street-Porter a year or two later when Ian brought me along to a recording of a TV show he was involved in, called *Around Midnight* (because that's the time it went out). A group of us went out for dinner afterwards and, on no evidence whatsoever, Janet decided I must be Ian's romantic companion, although I think the word she used to him later was 'catamite'. I'm sure she still thinks that he is really as gay as a goose, but his secret is safe with her.

Some idiot thought it would be a good idea to bring back Van der Valk, the 1970s detective:

> Piet Van der Valk is still played by Barry Foster, his brows
> perpetually knotted and his eyes constantly on the lookout
> for a minion to shout at ... Still, Mother Teresa would be
> a bit miffed if she had to say lines like 'Somewhat prema-
> ture, these preparations?' Or 'Has she had any threatening
> correspondence?' Because the characters are supposed
> to be Dutch, the script appears to have been translated
> from English into a sort of all-purpose Euro-bilge ... So

people say things like 'Go well, Stefan' and 'It's a matter not without its ramifications, of course.' Almost every line cries out not to be quoted.

14 February 1992

Private Eye works, I think, because of loyalty. Everyone who works there ends up staying years and years. Adam Macqueen arrived as a teenage intern; now he's in his forties and he's chief reporter. I went to a lunch there a few years ago to celebrate a number of aligning birthdays, and I realised that of the twenty people around the table, the only person who had been there for less than fifteen years was the current intern. People don't leave to take other jobs, they either retire or die. And if they retire, as Dave Cash did, rather too early at the age of fifty-five, they never cease to regret it. Compare and contrast with the atmosphere at the *Daily Mail*. Corinna, the showbiz editor in the late 1980s, told me recently that she had once asked one of her hacks to retool a news story. 'Fuck off, you cunt' was his reply.

In 1992, a couple of months after the *Punch* column came to an end, I got a phone call from one Simon O'Hagan, the newly appointed sports editor of the *Independent on Sunday*. Would I like to come and write a funny sports column for him? A broadsheet! Respectability! Not much money! Of course I would.

Luckily for me, 1992 was an Olympic year:

Tomorrow it'll all be over. The last medals will have been won. The last Briton will have come 19th ... Only the free holidays and enormous lunches for members of the IOC committee will continue, reassuring us all that, for some people at least, the Olympic flame never dies ...

What has made the most indelible impression on me, though, is the sheer varieties of bodies we have seen in the past few weeks. Big bodies, short bodies, wiry bodies, huge muscly bodies – we've seen virtually everything. In fact, the only thing we haven't seen is a normal body like yours or mine. It's remarkable what you can do to the human frame with years of intensive training, carefully planned diets and absolutely no performance-enhancing drugs at all, good Lord no.

9 August 1992

I wrote my sports column for about eighteen months, between spring 1992 and autumn 1993, and it's probably fair to say that, in career terms, this was me at my pomp. I was writing three columns a week, another column once a month, and sundry other bits and bobs that turned up. I was thirty-two, single and earning £50,000 a year. I was also, at the time, a bit of a prick. I remember going out for lunch at about this time with my friend David Taylor (better known as the writer D. J.) and a mutual friend called Francis, for whom we had both worked a few years previously. Francis was thirty years older than us and had been a significant mentor in both our lives. We ate at a posh restaurant in Covent Garden, and I remember that I was full of myself and boasted pretty much unceasingly. I then had to leave early because I had to go and see a programme at three o'clock at BBC Television Centre. I thought everything was about me, but it wasn't. It was all about Francis, whom I never saw again, and who disappeared out of all our lives not long after. He smoked like a beagle and drank red wine as though it was a soft drink, so I'm guessing he did not make old bones. I had this one opportunity to thank him for all he had been and done for me, and I blew it.

Success, when it comes, seems pre-ordained, inevitable. Another mistake. Success is a function of talent, of course, but it relies much more on happenstance. It's also incredibly fragile. Men like Piers Morgan who have known no failure, or whose sheer bumptiousness has enabled them to whoosh past failure as though it's a broken-down car, are fated to remain pricks for the rest of their lives. But who would like to live in Piers Morgan's head? Who would want to live with that terrible face? Success is its own reward, but also its own punishment.

I only went into the *IoS* offices once, although I did occasionally go out to lunch in a pub with Simon O'Hagan. He became my friend, but when he was pushed upstairs to edit the newspaper's comment pages, I had no back-up. His replacement, who didn't know me from Adam, ended my column within seconds of being appointed, but he did offer me a weekly sport-on-TV column, which I should have taken but didn't, fearing the knock-on effect on my *Daily Mail* career. Fear! I was so afraid when I was younger. Maybe the prickishness was my way of dealing with it; or maybe it was my way of not dealing with it. You wear the mask, you try to hide from the world how terrified you are, only to find out later that they all knew anyway.

Also in 1992, the *Oldie* opened for business. This was the brainchild of Richard Ingrams, who had retired from the editorship of *Private Eye* in his early fifties and felt, not unreasonably, that there was a little more snap in the celery yet. I had met Richard once or twice over the years but had always been horribly tongue-tied in his company, as he was something of a hero of mine and what do you say to such people? You gurgle, you gasp, you grin inanely, you go off and weep in a corner. But the *Oldie*, aimed not necessarily at the old but at the old-at-heart, was something I really wanted to be involved in. Its main editorial policy was For God's Sake Not the Usual People. It was Richard who discovered that Edward Enfield, Harry's crotchety old dad, was a superb columnist in the making, and he employed me too, despite my abject gurgling at parties. My first contributions were in a column called Modern Times, where different people would explain in detail, for the benefit of those too old to find out for themselves, certain mysterious features of late twentieth century life. 'What is ... a Reebok?' was one of mine, as was 'What is . . . Karaoke?' You would never guess I was in my early thirties when I wrote these jeremiads, all of which have a tinge of the mobility scooter about them.

The *Oldie* started as a fortnightly, published in *Private Eye*'s off week, but that proved unsustainable, so with some new cash it relaunched in 1995 as a monthly. Now, finally, I was to get some regular work there. David Taylor and I had published, in 1990, a book called *Other People*, a series of fictional portraits of modern types based on a similar work from the 1950s. We did half each: David's were much more polished and novelistic, while mine were broader and more comic. The book was brought out by Bloomsbury, and sold so abjectly that it might just as well not have existed at all.* There's an author photograph of us on the inside back cover, trying to look cool. 'Young scribblers on the make,' said David. But one person had seen the book and liked it: Richard Ingrams. In 1995 he invited us to continue the series in his magazine. We each did about a dozen before we ran out of steam, and this is the one that always turns up in compilations of the magazine, possibly because it is based closely on real life. It describes (with changed names) my mother's disastrous second marriage, and she liked the piece so much she framed it and hung it up in her bathroom, possibly as a warning to herself never to do anything so stupid again.

> Angus and Jane are married, just. Since the Maida Vale flat was sold, Angus has skulked in his Gloucestershire cottage, while Jane has bought a smaller flat near the bookshop where she works. Occasionally they speak on the telephone. More frequently, they speak to each other's answering machines.
>
> When Angus and Jane married four years ago, their

---

* Someone from Bloomsbury once told David that it was the lowest-selling book in their history, with a total sale of 124. Beat that, James Patterson!

friends were delighted but surprised. Jane's first husband had been a powerful, charismatic man, possessed of narcissistic good looks and the morals of a virus. Fatally addicted to cliché, he had succumbed to an unusually acute midlife crisis in his forties and run off with his secretary.

Angus, by almost comic contrast, was short and rotund, always laughing, a bit of a character. Long widowed, he had survived thirty-five years in advertising by being a bit of a character, by always laughing, and by manipulating and manoeuvring behind the scenes with unsqueamish ruthlessness. Jane found the combination intriguing, and was willing to overlook his less-appealing physical attributes. She had been mourning the loss of her husband – last heard of in Los Angeles with his latest twenty-five-year-old Nigerian girlfriend – for too long. Angus was good company. And after three decades at the top of his profession, he was rich enough to keep her in a style to which she looked forward to becoming accustomed. Jane was bored with genteel poverty. She still had her St John's Wood flat, the last remaining prize of her divorce settlement, but even that would have to go soon.

'But why don't you just live with him?' trilled her daughters, when she told them that Angus had proposed. Jane could see the logic of their argument, and had no strong moral objection to the idea. But like Elizabeth Taylor, she had long since decided that she was the marrying kind. They put their flats on the market, and prepared for married life.

Jane cannot remember when she first began to entertain doubts, although she now realises that the three-day honeymoon may have been a clue. Immediately after their return, Angus flew to Hong Kong on an urgent business trip. Jane supervised the transfer of her own and Angus's belongings to the new flat.

Several beloved artefacts failed to survive the move. Her cat, angry at the disturbance, urinated over Angus's favourite armchair. These were stressful weeks for Jane. Out in Hong Kong, Angus's urgent business trip continued apparently indefinitely, all expenses paid.

When Angus finally returned, Jane found him less jolly and entertaining than of old. In public he remained the life and soul. At home he was morose and pedantic. At first their differences were trivial. He liked his tea brewed in a mug, to the strength and consistency of bitumen. She preferred a pot of Earl Grey. He objected to the smell of her cat's litter. She wished he would wash his handkerchieves more often. And so on.

But more fundamental disagreements threatened. Angus now spent most of his days at home. Neither his various consultancies nor his chairmanship of an up-and-coming agency seemed to stretch him terribly hard. Even so, he still expected Jane to cook him dinner every night. Tired after a long day at the bookshop, Jane watched as Angus shovelled the fruits of her culinary skills into his gaping maw. At night, as she lay in bed, she could still hear his furious chewing, and see in her mind's eye flecks of mashed potato splashed across his fleshy lips.

The sex was unfortunate. Perhaps physical attraction would have made a difference after all. Angus's changes of mood were becoming increasingly unpredictable. When Jane bought herself a new coat he trudged gloomily around the flat as though a close relative had died. Relations between Angus and the cat declined. The cat urinated in one of his shoes.

Jane was noticing more and more about Angus, and

liking less and less. When he washed up, which wasn't often, he never washed the lids of the saucepans, so that they gradually accumulated layers of grime. He was a hypochondriac, who became convinced that he had caught shingles from an insect bite, despite no physical evidence of shingles or, indeed, an insect bite.

Worst of all, he was a tightwad. Absurdly generous during their courtship, Angus now seemed determined to hang on to every penny. Before they married, they had agreed that each would be responsible for his or her own immediate expenses, and that Angus would cover the housekeeping. His income, though infinitely mysterious, was known to be by far the greater. Three months after the wedding, Angus proposed that Jane should pay half the housekeeping in future, as she was rich, and he was finding it hard to make ends meet.

Ah, so that was it, thought Jane. He's after my money. What a shame I haven't got any. Meanwhile Angus was warming to his theme. Why did they need a cleaning woman? Why did Jane bother to work at all? She didn't need the money. He would much prefer to have Jane at home with him all day, cooking all his meals, tending to all his needs ...

A week later Jane ejected Angus from the marital bed. The cat developed severe bruising on her lower abdomen, and hid whenever Angus was in the room. Angus spent every weekend in Gloucestershire, either alone or with his grown-up children. Jane heard a rumour that he had signed over most of his assets to them in the event of a divorce settlement. Fortunately their lawyers get on famously.

May 1995

6

A Bit Tatty Around the Edges

'The talk deals with disappointing sales, inadequate publicity, more than inadequate royalties, idiotic or criminal reviews, others' declining talent, and the unspeakable horror of the literary life.'

Edward Gorey, The Unstrung Harp, *on literary parties*

Within the space of a week in autumn 1993, I was fired from two of my three weekly columns: the sports piece in the *Independent on Sunday*, and the weekly chatty TV page in Saturday's *Daily Mail*. I didn't have a contract for either, so that was £700 a week I was suddenly worse off, which is £35,000 a year. It was the kick in the nuts I probably needed, but I was staggering around doubled up in pain for a long time afterwards.

Success is only ever fleeting in the freelance game, while failure seems to last for ever. Actually, failure is endemic to the writer's life, and how you cope with it will determine whether or not this really is the life for you. One day recently I started counting how many times I had been sacked from things, and when I reached the teens I quietly gave up. Freelances are always the first to go. Also, not everyone is going to like your stuff. It's nothing personal, except when it is, and then there's *nothing* you can do about it.

As it happens, my double sacking at the age of thirty-three was my first serious career reverse, although obviously not the last. Failures still bite at the age of sixty-one, but you recover more quickly. You lose weeks of useful worktime rather than months or years. In 1993 I kept working at the work I still had – because you can't not – but I didn't get my creative breath back for about nine months. At such times, for some reason, the image of Bob Dylan often slips into my mind, playing a terrible harmonica solo. Dylan has had many hit albums, too many to list, but he has also had some notable failures, albums that simply weren't much cop, despite all the time and effort put into them. When you release a new album I imagine you learn fairly swiftly whether or not it's as good as you think it is. (Because no one, even someone as shambolic as Dylan, is going to put out an album that they don't believe has *some* merit.) First the reviews come in; then the sales figures. If both are dreadful, you have to lift yourself out of the pit of gloom in which you find yourself, and start again. As Samuel Beckett said, 'Ever tried. Ever failed. No matter. Try again. Fail again. Fail better.'

Nine months after the double sacking, I felt more robust and considered myself open to offers. I spoke to David Thomas, former editor of *Punch*, now a jobbing freelance like the rest of us, and he suggested his literary agent, who happened also to be the literary agent of a couple of other friends of mine, Mitch and Simon. This was a good sign. As it happens, David, Mitch and Simon would all sack Patrick within the next twelve months, whereas I'm still with him twenty-five years later. I'm sure there's some sense to this somewhere, but I haven't been able to find it.

Patrick and I threw around some ideas, and the best we could come up with was a pop music book, called *The Records That Time*

Forgot. Patrick arranged a meeting with Richard Beswick of Little, Brown, who liked my writing but not the book idea, not entirely surprisingly. He had read the sports columns in the *Independent on Sunday*, however, and liked the ones about the terrible cricket team I ran. Was there not a book in that? You could do a cricket version of Nick Hornby's *Fever Pitch.*

Now there's an idea.

Within ten minutes we had a deal.

The only problem was time. This was August 1995. The book needed to be out, at the latest, by mid-summer 1996, not least because other people were sure to have had the same idea, and we had to get in first. If they squeezed the production schedule to the bare minimum, they would need a manuscript by April. This gave me eight months to write the book. Never having written a book by myself before, and not knowing how long it took, I said, yes, I can do that. There is much to be said for naïveté. There's also something to be said, when you are doing something you have never done before, for a tough deadline, one that has to be achieved, or all is lost.

Rain Men is inconsistent, a bit tatty around the edges, and some of it is positively embarrassing to me now. But it has a wild, youthful energy you can't fake. This energy came from the boiling ructions within the cricket team. I had been running the team since university in 1979 with my old friend and writing partner Harry Thompson. But we were two strong personalities, who had both had some professional success in recent years, and we now had very different ideas about the sort of cricket team we wanted. Harry had played every game the team had ever played, and given that we customarily had about thirty-five games a year, two per weekend, this was quite an achievement. He captained on Saturday, and his team were becoming ferociously good, on the back of new players, many of them scarily muscled South African bartenders, who sought victory at all costs. I captained on Sunday and my team was full of the old lags who had been playing for years and wanted a quieter life. We were becoming two teams in one, except that Harry played for both. The internecine strife was becoming intolerable, and indeed, two years after the publication of *Rain Men*, I took the old lags and we formed a breakaway team, which still plays today. But in 1994/5, the pain was real, the rage was intense, and the book was driven by both.

Writing books is a strange business. It's seen very much as the pinnacle of our profession, but unless lightning strikes, you'll be doing it for pennies rather than millions of pounds. Most of us are more likely to be run over by the 134 bus on the Archway Road than write a bestseller. Such money as you do receive, you generally get up front, as what they call 'an advance on royalties'. This is to keep you eating food and enjoying the occasional warm bath while you're writing the damn thing. When one of my books makes a modest splash, everyone assumes the money is flowing in and the champagne's on me. I have to explain that the advance, the money I have already received – usually in tranches, one on signing the contract, one on delivering the manuscript, one on publication day, and often a fourth on publication of the paperback edition – has to 'earn out', which is to say that I have to sell quite a lot of copies before I'll see a penny more. This could take two or three years, or in the case of one of my books, nearly a decade. I now think of the advance as the fee for the book, so that if by some miracle I pay off the advance with book sales and start earning real cash, I think of that as free money. This is the eleventh book I have written and four of the first ten have paid off their advances, which is a decent ratio. Some of the other books failed utterly and spectacularly. Overall, I have sold around 220,000 books in twenty-five years, which isn't bad, but it's nothing special. Every book you write you think, this is the one, this will make me a billionaire. It's lovely to look at all your books on a shelf and think, blimey, I wrote all those. But if you divided the money you have made from them by the hours you spent working on them, the figure you'd arrive at would be rather less than the minimum wage.

Another odd thing is that almost no writer ever looks at a book again once he has finished writing it. Occasionally you might be dragged screaming to a literary festival and asked to give a talk about it to eleven pensioners and a cat sitting in mufflers in an unheated municipal library in the middle of November. You'll open it up then, probably on the train going there, with fear in your heart. If you don't, you will quickly realise that almost everyone you encounter who has read the book, has read it more recently than you have. This can lead to problems, especially when someone says, do you remember the bit when so-and-so-and-so-and-so happens, and you have to smile and pretend you know what they are talking about.

My books are relatively short, because I prefer them that way, and most of them take between eight and ten months to write. Sometimes a writer will tell me about a book they have spent four or five years writing, and for me that's like staring into the abyss. Different sorts of minds, different sorts of people, and in the end, different sorts of books. These days I write too long and cut, taking out anything that doesn't quite measure up. This is how my great literary hero P. G. Wodehouse worked in his youth. When he was old and failing, he would write short and then pad it out, and you can really see the difference. As it happens, cutting out the stuff that doesn't quite work is the most enjoyable part of the whole process. Slash and burn! If it's shit, it has to go!

Talking of staring into the abyss, most writers starting a book experience what we might call 'book vertigo'. You've written, say, four hundred words. You feel quite proud of that. Only ninety-five thousand to go. Whoa! It's a bit like standing on top of the Leaning Tower of Pisa and finding yourself horribly tempted to throw yourself off and end it all now. I won't claim that this gets much better with experience, because it doesn't. But having written a book or two, you do gain a weird confidence in your ability to get the job done. Having started, you know you'll finish, just as long as you don't think too much about it. Do the next bit, do the bit after that, do the bit after that. Book vertigo never altogether disappears, but you learn ways of distracting your attention from it.

If it's so difficult, scary, time-consuming and poorly remunerated, why do so many people write books? According to the old saw, everyone has a book in them, and really nothing could be further from the truth. Some people have many books in them, while most people have no book at all. This doesn't necessarily stop them from writing them, and in some cases getting them published, and in a few cases getting favourable reviews from people who turn out to be their friends. Almost all writers have met people at parties who say, I'm going to write a book one day, as though it might be an amusing leisure activity, like washing the car. Although the mere utterance of this sentence is reason enough to turn round and go and talk to someone else, we are either more polite than that ('Tell me all about it') or more cruel ('Have you ever written anything longer than a note to the milkman?'). In fact, there is a 100 per cent correlation between saying 'I'm going to write a book one day' and never, ever writing that book.

The secret, which generally we keep to ourselves, is that for the imaginative introvert, writing books is about as much fun as you can have with your clothes on – or, at least, a ratty old dressing gown. Hours and hours spent in your own company, dreaming things up: what could be better? Many writers I know complain incessantly about the terrible pain and anguish they go through when writing a book, to which my response is always: well, why don't you get a proper job? Go to an office? Wear a suit all day instead of your ratty old dressing gown? They blanch at the mere thought of it.

Writing articles can be fun too, and you have the adrenalin rush of finishing it, submitting it and then forgetting all about it until it appears in the newspaper or magazine a short while later, when you get another adrenalin rush all over again. But as I get older, my deadline anxiety has become more pronounced. I could never write as many articles now as I did in my early thirties, when I was churning them out almost every day.

Writing books means you don't have to travel so frequently on the Adrenalin Express; instead you can chug along on the slow train to Dopamine, visiting every station on the line. To minimise book vertigo, go slowly and take each section as it comes. Never think of what you'll be doing next week, let alone next month, or even tomorrow. Just enjoy what you're doing today. But as the book grows and develops, you will find that there are two thresholds to pass. The first is Cracking It. This is the moment at which, although you may have no detailed idea of how it is going to pan out, you can see that you will have enough material for a book and it's just a matter of marshalling it properly. For me this usually happens between a third and halfway through, and I always crack open a bottle to celebrate. The second is Breaking the Back of It. This happens around two-thirds, maybe three-quarters of the way through, when you realise that you have the whole book in your head. In fact, there's nothing else in your head at all. Someone asks you to take the rubbish out and you mumble something and take a yogurt out of the fridge and go back to work, having failed to take the rubbish out. This is the best bit, for you if for no one else.

Most writers do all their research before they start writing, but I'm both too lazy and too impatient for that. Geoff Dyer says he prefers just to start writing, see what he's saying and then do the research later, if he needs to. He finds out what he has to say by writing it, and for him that's a large proportion of the fun. Same for me, really. Research only fills the gaps left by the imagination.

In fact, it hardly matters which way round you do it, because almost everything you write at the beginning will never make it into the book. That's as it should be. The book will change as you are writing it, and that's good as well. Writing isn't the best career choice for control freaks, although it can be a good cure for control freakery, which I'm not sure is entirely compatible with sound mental health. The book should have a life of its own, and if it doesn't, it will have no life at all.

For writing isn't really about writing. Writing is about rewriting, and editing. It's about what builders call 'making good'. The best work you will do on the book will be the 1 per cent change you make at the very end, which will almost certainly improve the book by between 15 and 20 per cent. Most of this, as you'd expect, is a matter of hard-won experience.

So, while writing this chapter, I changed the habits of a lifetime and took another look at *Rain Men*, my first solo book. If I were doing it again, I realised, about a fifth of it would have to go. Not that I would be doing it again. Every book you write reflects the time in which it was written, and the person you were when you wrote it. We all think of ourselves as serenely unchanging, as beacons of consistency in an uncertain world, and if you want to prove that wrong, the very best way is to read a book you wrote more than twenty-five years ago. Bloody hell! Who was that idiot? Whoever he was, he is long gone.

This book, the one you are reading, reflects who I am now. In three years I'll write a different book which will reflect who I will be then. And I have no idea what that will be because I have no idea who I am going to be then. Indeed, writing that book, whatever it is, will help me find out.

This is why writers reach the age of sixty, as I did not so long ago, and think, only now do I really know what I'm doing. And how many years have I got left? Forty? Twenty? Five? You look back at all the years in which you weren't writing books and think, what the hell was I up to? 'Living your life' is the obvious answer, and it's only by doing that that you build up enough ideas and material to write more books.

Rain Men came out in 1995, and did quite well. But it was four years before I produced a second book, *Brain Men*, and another six before the third book arrived. Why so long?

Brain Men was a great idea,* a book about quizzes from the point of view of someone who both went to a lot of pub quizzes as a punter (which I still do) and had started to write and present his own (which I also still do). But the book proved much harder to write than the first one.

For like many writers, I suffered an unexpected crisis of confidence. For four agonising months I wrote and rewrote the intro-duction, and in all that time I never really improved it at all. Now, I would know that if something you are trying to write is proving that intractable, you just move on, write something else. I also know, as I didn't know then, that it's often worth leaving the introduction until last, when you know what else is in the book and you can wrap it all up in the intro with a nice Christmassy bow. But without as ferocious a deadline as I had for the first book, I took nearly a year to write *Brain Men*. And when it came out, nothing happened.

The problem was simple, and I really should have thought of this earlier: where do you put it in the shop? If you're writing novels, it's easy. You go in fiction, under your surname, and anyone looking for it can find in a trice (or not, if it's not there). But for non-fiction, you have to think carefully about which shelf it is going to be on. *Rain Men* was straightforward: it went in sport, on the cricket shelf. *Brain Men*, which had wonderful reviews and tons of feature coverage, could only be found tucked away at the bottom of the games and puzzles section, which is very rarely anywhere but at the back of the shop, next to dictionaries. No one bought it. It came out in paperback with a different cover. No one bought that either. It remains my second lowest seller, and only because the lowest seller came out seventeen years later.

---

* And a great title, dreamt up by my partner Paula.

I once a met a man from Waterstone's, with whom I was making idle bookchat when I said, the problem with books is that every book that can be written has been written. 'Twice,' said the man from Waterstone's, gloomily. *Brain Men* was, for its time, quite original, so no one knew what to do with it. But that may not have been the real problem. There have been several books on quizzes since, and through my underworld contacts in publishing I have ascertained that none of them sold particularly well either. It may be that people just don't want to buy books about quizzes. A shocking thought to me, and maybe an obvious thought to everyone else.

The failure of *Brain Men* knocked me for six. I'd say it cost me three years of my creative life, which may not have been helped by the fact that in the year it came out, Paula and I had our first child. As everyone knows and tells you, new parenthood is astonishingly tiring. For several years I wandered around in a sleep-deprived fog, so perhaps it's not a great surprise that I didn't start another book until early 2004. I did change a lot of nappies, though, as well as watching a lot of old episodes of *Inspector Morse* on the telly, and falling asleep halfway through every one.

7

The Fallow Years

'The most depressing part of *Little Women* (1869) is not
when Beth dies but when Jo's short story wins a prize of
$100, reminding any fellow writers reading the book that
freelance rates have remained roughly stable *since the
reconstruction era.*'

Jennifer Morrow on Twitter

Scroll back once again to 1996, if you will. I have one remain-
ing TV review a week at the *Daily Mail*, I have my monthly pop
column at the *Spectator* and I am an occasional contributor to
Private Eye and the *Oldie*. I have also acquired a couple of monthly
magazine columns, a last-page funny one for a science-fiction-on-
TV magazine called *Dreamwatch*, and a last-page funny one for
Wisden Cricket Monthly, on the back of the success of *Rain Men*.
Life is good. So why am I feeling so insecure?

One of the odder aspects of the freelance life is that you will go
and in out of fashion. It has nothing to do with your performance or

even your personality: it's just the way the wind is blowing. When you're new and exciting, everyone wants a piece of you. When you have been around for a while, everyone grows a little bored with you. There is no actual difference in the quality of the material you're producing; in fact, your writing may even have improved. But that's not the point: when you fall out of fashion, it is just one of those things, and you have to take it on the chin, because there is little you can do about it.

When you fall out of fashion at the *Daily Mail*, however, it's especially brutal. No one returns your calls. If anyone does call you up, it's to give you a bollocking. Paul Dacre, the new editor, had probably called me 'a cunt' in conference, or even his favourite term: 'a cunting cunt'. Apparently there's a way back from mere cuntitude. But a cuntiform cunticity of cuntitudes is usually final. (Apologies for the swearing. If you don't like it, you're best advised to stay well away from any newspaper office.)

I saw the writing on the wall, and that writing said, 'You're useless'. Really, given my lack of empathy with the great leader, I had done well to survive so long since his appointment. Keep your head down, Berkmann. Step slightly out of the limelight. This policy has served me well, and not just at the *Mail*, for more than thirty years.

In 1996 Sue Douglas was appointed editor of the *Sunday Express*, and one of the first things she did in office was to ring me up and ask me to be the TV critic. I jumped from the *Mail* before I was blatantly tripped in front of an empty lift shaft. Sue had big plans for the *Sunday Express*. She was going make it younger, brighter and cleverer. She was, as she has always been, the supreme optimist. She was reckoning without the readers of that poor, grim, benighted paper.

Newspaper sales have been plummeting down that same empty lift shaft for as long as anyone can remember. Young people can't see the point of print, and gain all their information online. Only oldies like me still have newspapers delivered every morning. But even among a generally ageing newspaper readership, *Sunday Express* readers were older, poorer and more likely to own budgies than anyone else. They didn't want their paper to be younger or brighter. They wanted it dedicated to Complan, support stockings and cheap meals for one on special offer at Tesco. The paper's readers were literally dying of old age. They watched telly all day and loved Kirstie Allsopp. The few of them who survived into the 2010s voted for Brexit because they wanted their passports blue again.*

Sue had miscalculated. During the nine months she lasted as editor, she produced a wonderful newspaper, full of good people writing at the peak of their form. My TV reviews, at least, show a definite improvement from my last few years at the *Mail*. All the same jokes, of course, albeit in a slightly fresher order. But sales did not recover; in fact, they were falling even faster than before. So Sue was given the boot and the editor of the main *Daily Express*, a former monk called Richard Addis, took over the *Sunday* as well and turned it into a seven-day operation. Oddly enough, I had also known Richard of old. He had also done a stint as *Daily Mail* features editor, and I had had lunch with him a few times. Incredibly posh, rather ascetic, Richard was as far from the thuggish, large-pored stereotype of the *Daily Mail* executive as you can get. Indeed, his survival there had been widely considered a miracle. One of his executives called him 'Chance the Gardener' after the simpleton played by Peter Sellers in the film *Being There*, who rises to the US presidency despite knowing nothing about anything. It was a cruel nickname but oddly apposite. Richard always had that air of wanting to be somewhere else: possibly editing the *Times Literary Supplement*, or getting out of bed to start praying at half past four every morning.

One thing he never had a problem with, though, was making

---

* Have you noticed how all the people who wanted blue passports back don't actually go abroad, because it's full of foreigners?

decisions. One of his first was to ring me up to fire me from the TV critic's job on the *Sunday Express*. He explained that he had taken the astoundingly pompous former broadsheet journalist Anthony Holden out to lunch and asked him if there was any job he would like on the paper. Holden stroked his fat, purulent chin for a second or two and then said he would like my job. It's yours, said Richard. Which I can understand, but why tell me that? It's bad enough that I'm losing the column, but what variety of moron do you have to be to give me the full story?

Richard then offered me another job. He was planning to move the sports coverage from the back of the paper to an eight-page pull-out supplement in the middle, and he wanted me to write a daily sport-on-TV column. Realising that such a job would have me in a padded cell within three months, I said no, and he then gave me a once-a-week funny sports column, of precisely the same type I had written for *Punch* and the *Independent on Sunday*. I said yes, and he offered me a year's contract, the second and last newspaper contract I have ever signed. I don't like contracts at all, so I can't have trusted him an inch.

Of my year writing dismal unread sports columns in a dismal unread newspaper, little need be said. More than once I went to parties and people asked me whether I was still a journalist. No, I said, I'm writing for the *Daily Express*, and they looked at me as though I had died. It is the only job I have ever done purely for the money.

If I have a personal philosophy as a freelance, it's that you must always remember the Freelance Triangle. When anyone rings you up to offer you a job, you need to consider the three apexes of the Freelance Triangle. Is there any money in it? Is there job satisfaction? Is there kudos? If your answer to two of the three questions is yes, then you should go ahead. If your answer to only one of the three is yes, then you should politely decline. There are no jobs that give all three. Well, there has been one, but we'll talk about that later.

So, for example, if a job is cool but the money is feeble and you're going to be bored to death doing it, then you say no. It's a really helpful formulation, and it has got me out of trouble on more than one occasion.

I was right to sign the *Express* contract, because it rapidly became clear that no one on the paper, from Richard Addis down, gave a flying fuck what I was writing. I was almost surprised to get a phone call, near the contract's end, from an astoundingly rude man who told me, in between furious sips of coffee, that next week's column would be my last. They can't even fire you politely in Fleet Street. I think you're supposed to feel grateful that you haven't been impaled on giant spikes instead of being given your P45.

That seemed to be it for me and newspapers. For the first time in a decade, I was adrift.

It was scary, and at the same time liberating.

In the years since, I have occasionally bumped into graduates of the *Daily Mail* school of hard knocks, all of whom had the same thing to say, although they said it in very different ways. You could have been a contender. You could have been a star of the *Daily Mail*. You could be up there now in the top tier, earning two hundred grand a year, and eating enormous lunches every day. Two enormous lunches, if you felt like it.

And very patiently, I have had to explain why that could never have been so.

One reason is that as I have grown older, I have become much more left wing. Here's a list of the ways I have voted since my first general election, the Margaret Thatcher coronation of 1979, when I was eighteen:

1979: Conservative.
1983: SDP. (I was a founder member. I've even got the certificate somewhere.)

1987: SLD. (The Social and Liberal Democrats, or the Salads, as they were known.)
1992: Didn't vote. Too angry and disillusioned.
1997: Labour. (Tony Blair. It was compulsory.)
2001: Labour.
2005: Liberal Democrat. (Because Tony Blair went into Iraq. I could not vote for him ever again.)
2010: Liberal Democrat. (I liked Gordon Brown but I liked our Lib Dem MP more.)
2015: Labour. (Our Lib Dem MP turned out to be a Tory stooge.)
2017: Labour. (We now had an excellent Labour MP. Her swing was the largest towards Labour in the entire country.)
2019: Labour.

When David English was editing the *Daily Mail*, it was already voraciously right wing, but showbiz, as he said, was the heart of the paper. Paul Dacre shifted that balance, and made right-wing politics the heart, soul, liver, lungs and spleen of the paper. You can only fake things to a certain extent, and I realised I had found my limit quite early on.

The second reason I was never going to make it at the *Mail* is that I wasn't a Paul Dacre person. Nothing to do with politics. Just temperamentally.

And the third and most crucial reason, which underpins this entire memoir, is that I'm an introvert. I spend a lot of time by myself, and in truth I'd like to spend even more time by myself. The best definition of an introvert I have encountered is this: someone who expends energy being with other people, and recharges only in his or her own company. An extrovert is the opposite: recharges in the company of others, finds it tiring, even stressful, to be by themselves.

Journalism is an extrovert trade. You can't be afraid of making phone calls, of meeting people, of asking the difficult question, of putting yourself out there. That's not a description of me. If I have a difficult phone call to make, I can delay making it for weeks, possibly for ever. As it happens, there are no easy phone calls.

Weirdly, I once had an argument with the actress Maureen Lipman about this, after an *Oldie* lunch. She said she thought that shyness was mere arrogance. I said it might seem like that to an instinctive, effortless extrovert, especially in a world that essentially rewards the fearless and outgoing over those like me who would rather sit in a room and read a book than do anything else at all, but she was too cross to listen, which extroverts often are, I find. (Or did I say that? Did I, in truth, say absolutely nothing and merely formulate the sentence in my mind several hours later? Introverts are good at that.)

A couple of conversations that I had with ex-*Mail*ers about my 'failure' to make it big ended rather unpleasantly. Why did they care so much? I think they were angry because they felt I didn't care enough, that I didn't love the paper as fervently as they did. They were right: I didn't. I was always one of nature's freelances, light of spirit and bright of underpants.

Still, by 1997 things weren't going exactly swimmingly, which was why I had so much time to write *Brain Men*. There was also money to worry about. For the next three years I earned very little. At the time I thought, well, I have my freedom, but these three years of low earnings took twenty years to recover from.

Wherever two or three freelances gather together, you can be reasonably confident that they will talk about money. In fact, based on many such meetings in an absurd number of pubs, I can say that freelance writers have several obsessive subjects of conversation:

- Money.
- Their agents/publishers/commissioning editors and how useless they all are.

- Awards they haven't won or been shortlisted for (i.e. all of them).
- Their friends.
- Their enemies. (There's often a large overlap between these last two groups.)

But money is the big one. We never have enough, and we always want more. It's not a particularly fascinating conversation, although it is to us. And this despite the fact that we have willingly chosen a profession, trade, art or craft in which almost everyone is atrociously underpaid. What else were we expecting? J. K. Rowling's hundreds of millions?

(Actually, scratch the skin of any writer and you will find that they *were* expecting J. K. Rowling's hundreds of millions, and they take it as a personal insult that she got them and they didn't.)

I haven't done too badly financially over the years. I have never made £60,000 in a year, although I have got close once or twice. But every freelance career, however lucrative, is going to feature some failure along the way, and when it does, you need to be prepared for at least a year or two of penury, during which you will spend your savings (if any), stop taking taxi cabs and see your credit card bills mount to terrifying proportions. As previously mentioned, I also chose this time of my life to embark on parenthood, which is so expensive I might just as well have put down a non-returnable deposit on a Saturn V rocket and been done with it. Some freelance careers never recover from this phase. I know several people who had to go out and get proper jobs to pay their bills, and that was it: their dream had died. I was made of sterner stuff, although the fact that I had no transferable skills whatsoever and was therefore as employable as a lamb cutlet may also have had something to do with it.

What do we do when the work dries up? We try something else. After *Brain Men* came out, I spent the best part of two years trying to write a screenplay, with a co-writer, for a romantic comedy set in the glamorous milieu of north London pub quizzes. Richard (yet another Richard) had directed a lot of television drama and a handful of films, and wanted to get into writing. I didn't have anything else to do. It was the perfect combination. We wrote seventeen drafts, of which the ninth was undoubtedly the best, and even that wasn't close to being good enough. We were lucky enough to be bankrolled throughout by a production company, although the term 'bankrolled' suggests piles of lovely money, thrown at us in wads. In fact, hour for hour, I have never worked for less. We could go to parties and claim truthfully that we were writing a screenplay, but we were earning less than the waiters at those parties, less than the people who washed up afterwards, and only slightly more than the tramps lying under their sleeping bags on the street outside trying to get some sleep. I learned several important lessons in this time. One, that screenwriters really are the lowest of the low in the film world. No one smiles at you, or catches your eye. It's de rigueur for producers to treat you with contempt, possibly because if they didn't, you might ask them for more money. Our producer was always in a meeting, or going to a meeting, or coming back from a meeting, whereas I think we knew in our heart of hearts that he was just sitting in Starbucks doing the *Daily Telegraph* crossword.*

The second thing I learned was that I'm not a screenwriter. I can do the jokes, but plot and character always remained frustratingly out of reach. Richard, it turned out, was quite good at plot and character, but he had very little sense of humour, and really wanted to make a gritty, Ken Loach-style exposé of the misery of young Londoners caught up in the murky underworld of lousy quiz questions. Our friendship, and our scripts, began to suffer. We started

---

* At one of our terrible meetings, another possible producer turned up who I recognised, because he had been in the year above me at school. To try to break the ice I told him this, and for the first and indeed last time in the meeting he looked me in the eye. His glare of contempt was a bit like a phaser, set to kill. It meant, 'You are mistaken. I could never have been at school with a screenwriter.'

writing drafts separately, and less well. He gave up directing films altogether and became a life coach. It was all a complete disaster.

Not wasted, though, for nothing ever is. I learned a lot from Richard, mainly about telling stories, and I found that when I next came to write a book, I had a narrative arc for it in my head that wouldn't have been there but for the screenwriting. Richard and I meet up from time to time for a drink and wonder what went wrong. We were failing again, I usually say. Failing better.

8

Who Painted the *Mona Lisa*?

'Magazines all too frequently lead to books, and should be regarded as the heavy petting of literature.'

Fran Lebowitz

In 1999 Ian Hislop had an idea. It was for a short column, to be called Dumb Britain, that would collect real but boundlessly stupid answers to quiz questions on radio and TV. I wasn't sure about the title – I'm still not sure about it – but the idea was fantastic. Someone else edited it for a while, but whoever it was didn't do it as well as Ian wanted them to. Then he remembered *Brain Men*, which had made it palpably clear that I was a quiz nutter of serious proportions. The first Dumb Britain editor was quietly jettisoned and I was hired in their place. I have now been running this column for twenty years.

Dumb Britain is what we in the trade call a cushy number. People send them in, I look at them, I choose four to go in the magazine and I get paid for it. A trained gibbon could do the job.

Over the years I have also edited a few tiny paperbacks that have collected the year's best Dumbs, although these days Ian just picks the best of the year's output himself and gives them a page in the *Private Eye* Annual. Astoundingly, though, the column carries on, because quiz shows carry on, and people keep going on quiz shows despite not knowing anything at all. For instance:

Graeme Garden on *Beat the Nation*, Channel 4: What is the highest mountain in England?

Contestant, after long pause: Everest.

Anne Robinson on *The Weakest Link*: What is the highest mountain in Scotland? Ben ... what?

Contestant: Everest.

Eamonn Holmes on *National Lottery: Jet-Set*: Ben Nevis is situated in which mountain range?

Contestant: The Himalayas.

Anne Robinson again: The Suez Canal links the Red Sea with which other body of water?

Contestant: The Thames.

Anne Robinson again, several months later: Into what body of water does the river Thames flow?

Contestant, after long pause: The Atlantic.

All of which shows that quiz shows ask many of the same questions over and over again, and that people are forever finding new and dafter ways of getting them wrong.

Why do people do this? Oddly enough, I had the inside track on this because my friend Esther, who I met at university and was one of the cleverest people I have ever known, went on *Trivial Pursuit* on BBC1 in the 1980s. She described the process perfectly. The man asks you a question and your brain knows the answer. But somewhere between your brain and your mouth something goes badly wrong, for your mouth, which knows little about anything, confidently gives the wrong answer. I myself went on *Fifteen to One* on Channel 4, and William G. Stewart – who, like all the best game show hosts, managed to be amiable and faintly menacing at the same time – asked me this: Which French king, known as the Sun King, was fond of dancing and singing but saw no point in reading? And I knew: it was Louis XIV. But again, in the two and a half inches between thinking organ and speaking organ, there was a catastrophic system-wide failure. My mouth said 'Louis XVI'. Well, I was only two out. Half a point for trying?

Quiz shows proliferate these days because they are popular and cheap to make. Alexander Armstrong and Richard Osman on *Pointless* may look expensive, and the set shimmers and shines, but they are shooting four episodes a day, and you can do a whole month's run in a longish weekend. When Max Bygraves was hosting *Family Fortunes* back in the 1980s, he would insist that they shot the entire run, twenty-six episodes, in one go. It took less than a week. If it's Tuesday it must be the Bridlington family from Blackpool. Or possibly the Blackpool family from Bridlington.

Dumb Britain is therefore a bit of a misnomer. We're not saying, you're a bad person for being so thick, the whole country's dumbing down and going to the dogs. We're not saying that at all. We're saying, why on earth did you go on this programme when you don't know anything?

Quiz shows demonstrate, as no other television can, that most people are at heart optimists. They think they'll muddle through somehow. They won't make the mistakes that everybody else makes. They're not stupid. Unfortunately, only the truly clever realise and acknowledge how stupid they are. As the career of Donald Trump has shown, the truly stupid are too stupid to realise how stupid they are.

This has been going for some time. This one was from Radio Merseyside, sometime in the 1970s or 80s:

Presenter says: What was Hitler's first name?

And the caller says: Heil.

A lot of the most famous ones come from *Family Fortunes*, whether presented by Max Bygraves or not. On *Family Fortunes* you could get whole dynasties of the dim.

> Name a type of fork not used for eating.
> Guy Fawkes.

They are among my favourites because the thought processes involved are so surreal.

> Name something sold by gypsies.
> Bananas.

> Name a part of the body everyone has only one of.
> First contestant said, big toe.
> Second contestant said, wedding tackle.
> Third contestant said, combine harvester.

I have long wondered whether there's an ur-Dumb, the first ever Dumb that engendered all the other Dumbs, the Adam and Eve of Dumbs. If the latter, it was the serpent in the Garden of Eden who was asking the questions.

Here's one from *3-2-1* in 1978, presented by Ted Rogers, with his (even then) unfeasibly purple hair.

Ted: This is a composer, German by birth, English by adoption,

best known for an oratorio published in 1741. [beat] It was called ...
Messiah. [two beats] You're bound to know ... his handle.

BZZZ! Both teams press buzzers. A woman on one team
was first.

So who is it, says Ted.

The woman shuts her eyes: Oh God, I used to have it at
school ... Handel's *Water Music* ...

So who's the composer?

Chopin?

The audience goes mental. Ted turns to the other team: So I can
offer it to you.

And the team captain shakes his head and says: Beethoven?

For many years the column owed a grave debt to *The Weakest
Link*, hosted with visible contempt by Anne Robinson. Contestants
were cowed into idiocy, although it could just have been that they
couldn't quite hear what Anne was saying and were therefore
answering completely different questions.

> Which German painter was famous for his portraits of
> Henry VIII? Hans ...
>   Solo.

> What was the principal language used by ancient Romans?
>   Greek.

> Which hot drink is an anagram of the word 'eat'?
>   Hot chocolate.

> What 'R' is the westernmost island of the British Isles?
>   Argyll.

> Who was the first King of England to speak on the radio?
>   Henry VIII.

The humorous verses 'Oh I wish I'd looked after me teeth' and 'They should have asked my husband' were written by which British poet?

Tennyson.

The only criterion for publishing is that it's funny. I occasionally get letters from people asking us to print the correct answers, but that's not the point of the column. I don't care what the right answer is, as long as the wrong answer makes you laugh. For instance, another one from *The Weakest Link*:

The food colouring E110 is also known as sunset what?

Well, I wouldn't know. I'd guess yellow. I looked it up on Wikipedia and that's the right answer. But the answer definitely isn't what the contestant said, which was: Boulevard.

It was funny, so it went in.

With some Dumbs, you can work out what happened. Sometimes the question is being read out, and at some point the contestant simply stops listening. So Anne asks:

What surname was shared by a historical outlaw called Butch and a fictional cowboy called Hopalong?

And the contestant answered: Lesbian.

He had heard 'butch', but nothing after that. He couldn't stop himself saying 'lesbian'. Like an iron filing to a magnet, it was impossible to resist.

Sometimes, though, it's just pure lack of knowledge.

Eamonn Holmes, *National Lottery: Jet Set*, asks: Who wrote *The Catcher in the Rye*?

Contestant says: Chaucer.

On LBC, the presenter asks: Which French author has been translated into more languages than any other French author in the world?

Contestant says: Chaucer.

And Anne Robinson again: The British composer of the *Sea Symphony* and the opera *The Pilgrim's Progress* was Ralph Vaughan ... what?

Contestant says: Chaucer.

Are they all real? Just occasionally one comes in that doesn't smell right, and I discount it. Increasingly I get them from the people who actually make the programmes, which is helpful. When there was a new book out, I would do interviews with local radio stations, and someone would always say, I've got a brilliant one for you. Some they had been keeping for years for this very eventuality.

The best ones you know are real because no one could make them up. A useful source for a while was a now forgotten Sky show called *Are You Smarter Than a Ten-Year-Old?* The answer was usually no.

Host: What does five squared equal?

Grown-up contestant: In my day it was five times five, but I wonder if it may be the same as five cubed now.

Or this one on TalkSport:

Which Scotsman discovered penicillin in 1928?

Alexander Penicillin.

Fancy asking a TalkSport listener who invented penicillin. It's almost cruel.

My two favourite Dumb Britains. The first was on Radio 1 a few years ago. Sara Cox asked: Complete this well-known phrase. 'Beauty is in the eye of the ...' And the caller thought for a moment and said: Tiger. Which, I think, has a form and a perfection all of its own.

That would be my runner-up. My champion of champions was on *The Weakest Link*, again a long time ago. Anne Robinson asked: Who painted the *Mona Lisa*? And the contestant replied, Frank Bough.

It was several months before I worked that one out. Obviously the contestant knew the name of only one artist, Van Gogh. And somewhere in his mind, the man who painted *Sunflowers* and the knitwear-crazed former host of *Grandstand* and *BBC Breakfast Time* had become conflated. The point is, the intellectual processes required to reach the answer 'Frank Bough' are infinitely more complex and interesting than any you'd use to answer the question correctly.

In the early 2000s I was still doing the occasional TV review for the *Eye* while Square Eyes was in rehab or on holiday, but even I knew I was running out of road. As someone who had once watched television constantly and assiduously, I was now watching it occasionally and reluctantly. So Ian shifted me away from that and into the books department. His Literary Review page had a very simple job: obliteration by means of heavy satire. You can let rip in this column because all contributions are anonymous, although I generally didn't mind if people knew it was me, unless it was a book by someone I knew, in which case I would say nothing at all, and deny it vigorously if I bumped into them at a party.

Here's the *Eye*'s judgement of Sharon Osbourne's first memoir, *Extreme*, which sold 656,000 copies, all now available at your local charity shop:

> Once we're into the book proper, Sharon gets down to business: boasting how rich she is. 'I have more chandeliers than most people have light bulbs,' she says early on, maintaining a one-boast-per-page ratio with the single-mindedness that has shaped her long and terrifying career . . .

It's not a happy life. 'I light the most expensive candle I have to hand ... Burning money is about the only way I know to feel good about myself.' Sharon isn't just very much richer than you, she's more miserable too. 'I want to wake up in the morning and not feel terrified of the knock on the door' (page 49). 'I sometimes wonder what my life would have been like if I had bonded with my mother' (page 34). After several gruesome pages describing her abortion, she reveals that the only person she had to talk to afterwards was her cat. These days it's her dog. She has come a long way.

And so it goes on, an incontinent gush of therapy-scented bilge, interspersed with tales of what an evil bastard her dad was. Some of it is beyond parody. 'From downstairs I can hear "Touch Me And I Bleed" ... Ozzy's rock opera about Rasputin is finally coming together, and it's fucking brilliant.' It's also transcendentally vulgar, several facelifts beyond anything the rest of us could muster. 'By this time I'm laughing so much, I'm wetting myself, so holding my crotch I run for the door, my hand already soaking.' Poor bladder control becomes one of the book's more memorable motifs. You'd think twice about inviting the Osbournes round to dinner, unless your dining room was unusually well drained.

14 October 2005

The way we choose the books for review never changes. Ian and I separately look around for something we think might be useless. I then buy it and read it, and if it's as useless as we thought it would be, I review it. On occasion, I have rung up Ian and said, this book is actually quite good. So then we shelve it and move on to something else.

Not in October 2006, though. In a stroke of magnificent

serendipity, Gordon Ramsay and Marco Pierre White published memoirs within days of each other.

Is it a coincidence? No sooner does one roaring behemoth of modern cooking publish his warts 'n' more warts autobiography, than the other one, stamping his vast feet in the primeval swamp, publishes his too. There they stand, rending the air with their cries, tearing up trees with their bare paws and then lightly sautéeing them, maybe with some caramelised leeks on the side. Which one will win? Does anyone care?

Marco Pierre White is the elder of the two and the only one to flaunt a phallic cigar on his front cover ... No one in world history has worked harder. 'When I turned seventeen on 11 December 1978 I had a day off, but I still went into work.' Twenty-hour days were routine. 'I could take the bollockings because I had been toughened up by my childhood.' Having taken them, he then dishes them out to the poor bastards he hires to work for him. 'In order to achieve my dream I reckoned I needed a brigade with army-standard discipline and, as I learned at Gavroche, discipline is born out of fear.' Otherwise he is generally settling scores with the many thousands of individuals he seems to have fallen out with, all of whom did Marco wrong. It's a bizarre book – long, solipsistic, operatically boring, less of an autobiography than a psychological case history ...

Gordon Ramsay, five years younger, was a protégé of White's and in some senses could now be said to have surpassed him. Certainly in the publishing sense, for this is Ramsay's tenth book, albeit his first without recipes. Like White, he endured a terrible childhood: his father was a violent, alcoholic tyrant, and Ramsay feels he could easily have gone the same way as his younger brother, who ended up a heroin addict. Instead he went the same way as Marco Pierre White. No one in world history has worked harder. 'I'm as driven as any man you'll ever meet. I can't ever sit still. Holidays are impossible.' And nothing he does ever satisfies him. 'I still see a little boy who is desperate to escape, and anxious to please.' Reading these books back to back is a little like having a recurring nightmare. 'She was amazing – though we don't talk now, it all ended rather badly.' Of course it did: for these men it always does.

Ramsay's book, though, is much less revealing than White's: it's shorter, more guarded, more carefully edited. Some parts of his personal history he races through as though he has a train to catch. As in life, his regular use of the F-word sometimes feels a little studied, as though we all know that Gordon's a bit like that, so there has to be at least one a page, even though it might stand out as slightly fucking unnecessary. There are some typically sensitive bons mots: 'Before I met Jackie, I used to feel that sex was like sharpening a pencil. You stick it in there, and grind it around.' All the ghost's care cannot conceal his subject's monumental self-regard, or his very particular attitude to women. Of two relationships he writes, 'Why did Tana succeed where Ros had failed?' In other words, he was the catch: if the relationship didn't work it was the woman's fault. Very little, we get the impression, is ever Gordon's fault.

13 October 2006

I have done some of my best work for *Private Eye*, and also some of my worst. I think that's because the tone of Literary Review is so difficult to keep up: relentless disdain can be a little one note.

When it works it's glorious. When it doesn't quite, it's like a macaw screeching into your ear. It all depends on how much there is to say, and how much there is to say depends entirely on the book.

Everyone, though, finds their level, and mine was the auto-biographies of the famous, the psychopathic, the deluded, the egomaniacal, the borderline dangerous and William Shatner. Even the most guarded and careful of books, like Cliff Richard's, yielded up goodies if you looked hard enough for them. What, then, of the 'h' that dare not speak its name? (No, not holiness.)

> Cliff races through the early years of his career as though he has a prior engagement. So long has he been polishing these anecdotes, you suspect he can no longer remember the actual events. Within a chapter or so he's a global megastar (except in the US), contemplating conversion to Christianity and moving in with his 'manager' Bill. At last, we think, the nitty gritty.
>
> In fact, he proves as evasive as ever. If he'll admit to anything, it's low-level heterosexuality: he tells us about some early girlfriends and lets us know how attractive he finds the women of Paris, stopping short of saying 'Phwoarr!' But he does keep mentioning homosexuality, if only to say he hasn't a problem with it. After a while you find yourself trying to decode the most innocent sentences. 'I've always been a coward when it comes to telling people things I know they won't want to hear.' Such as your fans that you are a friend of Dorothy? 'I rented an apartment in Florida recently and before I left I couldn't resist going through it with a vacuum cleaner.' Not that anyone would suggest that a lifelong love of housework is an indicator of sexual preference; nor is the admission that he once played Bottom in *A Midsummer Night's Dream*. But because he tells you so little with his actual words,

he effectively coerces you to read between the lines. He also, unwittingly, gives us a splendid new euphemism for Ugandan relations: 'After a long session of theological argument and discussion I would often stay the night with him and his mother in Finchley . . .'

In between he rants on and on about British radio's refusal to play his new songs, and his continuing inability to break America. And it gradually dawns on the reader that celebrity memoirs are now all but interchangeable: the tough childhood, the 'hard but fair' psychotic dad, the early years of success dimly remembered, the houses in Barbados, the famous friends, the grudges borne against 'the media', the endless gnawing hunger for validation. Maybe the enormous cheque he will receive for this book will help with this latter, but don't bet on it.

3 October 2008

Eventually, one of the legs fell off our sofa (probably too much rocking small children to sleep), and rather than replace the entire sofa, I put a variety of terrible books I had reviewed for *Private Eye* under there to hold the damned thing up. *Westlife: The Autobiography* was there, as was Ian Botham's third memoir, and one by a Nolan Sister. They all performed much more admirably as a sofa leg than they ever had as works of literature.

9

Sheer Joy

'Art is the only work open to people who can't get along with others and still want to be special.'

Alasdair Gray, Lanark

In 1999 I was at a low ebb. Thrust aside by Fleet Street, latest book not selling, writing a not-very-good screenplay, earning buttons, and not even forty! But Richard Ingrams, first and greatest editor of the *Oldie*, came to my rescue, and made me his film critic, even though I had never reviewed films before, or maybe because of that. It was wonderful to have a regular gig at one of my favourite magazines, even though most of the other contributors were well struck in years and I wasn't even forty. Which for some reason didn't seem to matter any more.

Richard proved to be rather laissez-faire as an editor. His philosophy was to do as little as possible and wait for things to happen. He would no more tell me which films to review than instruct me which socks to wear in the morning. This seemed an admirable attitude to me, and from the start I was able to write the film column I wanted to write, which wasn't the same as all the others. Most film critics go and see films before they come out, in preview theatres, sometimes weeks or months before release, and their job is to be bang-up-to-the-minute, telling their readers about what's out this week and whether or not they should go and see it. Whereas I figured that *Oldie* readers weren't in so much of a hurry. My plan was to go and see films when they were already out, in cinemas surrounded by normal people. This gave me several advantages: one, that I had already read the reviews, so I knew which films to see and which to miss; two, that I could eavesdrop on the punters in the cinema, which often provided excellent copy; and three, that I didn't have to supply long passages of exposition explaining what the film was about, because chances are the readers already knew. It was, in short, the Very Lazy Film Critic's approach to reviewing films. It sustained me for nearly two decades.

The *Oldie* has had several proprietors, countless deputy editors and (so far) three editors, but it has long had a benign attitude to its writers, who are generally invited to at least two or three magnificent parties every year. The pay may be modest, but the hospitality is superb. I think Richard and his business manager, James Pembroke, understood instinctively that the best magazines are like clubs, for writers and for readers. If everyone feels they belong to this club, they will give you their hearts and souls, and only very rarely ask you for more money. Or never ask you for more money, in my case.

I fell into a routine. I'd usually go and see a couple of films on the Friday, one of them of my own choosing, and one I thought would appeal to the *Oldie* readership more than it might to me. (The film I wasn't so interested in was almost always better than the one I really wanted to see.) I'd write the review up over the weekend and deliver on Monday lunchtime at 610 words, which fitted the space allocated, but gave the subs a few words to cut if they so desired. (All subs so desire.)

> *American Beauty* is directed by a young Englishman, Sam Mendes, who is renowned for being both highly talented and very, very lucky. Not every first-time director gets a shot at a script as good as this one. The writer is Alan Ball, which is his own private tragedy, and we must not dwell on it – but my, can he structure a screenplay.
>
> *March 2000*

As though to show that no work is ever wasted, this was about halfway through my own doomed attempt to structure a screenplay. I could see when someone else did it well; I just couldn't do it myself.

I went to see *Mission: Impossible 2*, which gave me just the excuse I needed to ramble on about the original TV series:

> Thirty years or so ago *Mission: Impossible* was a rip-roaring 1960s TV spy series which introduced to Western civilisation the phrase 'this tape will self-destruct in five seconds'. Each week for eight years and 174 episodes, the prematurely white-haired Jim Phelps and his sidekicks managed to capture the microfilm, overthrow the South American dictator or bring the mob boss to trial, all in the space of fifty breathless minutes. While undeniably repetitive, the show had a style and a coherence all its own, as well as possibly the best theme tune of all time. As an eight-year-old I was particularly impressed by the scene at the beginning of each show in which, after the tape had self-destructed, Phelps returned to his groovy penthouse flat, sat on a leather sofa idly smoking a ciga-rette and leafed through a file full of photos of his various

operatives, before choosing the same four every time because they were the other four stars of the show.

August 2000

That piece ended with the sentence 'This review will self-destruct in five seconds.'

> To be obsessed with the wigs of the famous, as I seem to be, is to be constantly distracted by wigs. Paul Simon is a much revered and loved songwriter, but it's hard to take anyone seriously who walks around with *that* on his head. It's the same with Bruce Willis, a notoriously hair-free Hollywood star whose recent films have been notable for the luxurious mops that have adorned his gleaming skull. In *Armageddon* he saved the world from a vast meteor. Hundreds of millions of dollars were spent on special effects, yet there was only one special effect I could see, and it was probably stuck on with UHU.
>
> *February 2001*

What may, or may not, come over in these brief excerpts, but is clearly apparent from the full pieces, is the sheer joy I had in writing them. I don't remember this joy at the time – I was, as ever, too nervous about getting fired – but for a lot of writers, the more freedom they are given, the better work they will do. Richard Ingrams, if he liked you, gave you complete freedom. While I trusted that he liked me, I wanted nothing better than to please him. When you have an editor who you know is on your side, you're only ever writing for an audience of one.

> *Bridget Jones's Diary*, as all the world knows, is based on Helen Fielding's mountainously successful comic novel . . .

[Renée] Zellweger's accent is sure enough, although she struggles with the rhythms of British English, which must be as alien to her as black pudding for breakfast. There's also the issue of her weight gain, for Bridget in this film reveals what no actress has voluntarily made public in living memory: cellulite ...

And yet despite this cellulite, and her endless complaints at being unable to find a man, Bridget is pursued by Hugh Grant and Colin Firth, heart-throbs both. She also lives in Southwark in an extraordinarily photogenic flat, which means she can walk to work each day through an old-fashioned fruit and vegetable market peopled by extras who are obviously dying to cry 'Luvverly apples! Only a shilling a pound!' and sing songs from *My Fair Lady*. Drinking like a chimney and smoking like a fish, she also has a coterie of Quirky Best Friends with whom she regularly eats in expensive restaurants. It's not a bad life, however you look at it. Indeed, her greatest problem throughout the film seems to be a slightly greasy nose.

May 2001

Any film about Alzheimer's was pretty much compulsory. I trooped off to see *Iris* with a sinking heart, but was pleasantly surprised.

The acting is excellent. Kate Winslet [who played the young Iris] has been lampooned by the newspapers for not having read any of Murdoch's books, but so what? Her clever, sexually adventurous but oddly innocent Iris is enormously appealing, and her bare buttocks will gladden the hearts of many an Englishman.

March 2002

I kept going, as all columnists do, although after a decade or so Richard Ingrams began to wonder whether he needed a film critic at all. Didn't everyone just watch DVDs these days? I disagreed and waited to be fired. But Richard, as well as having the lowest boredom threshold of anyone I have ever met, also dislikes confrontation, so he started cutting all the jokes out of my pieces and waited for me to resign in a rage. One of the staffers on the magazine told me this in the strictest confidence, and also told me that after Richard had done this, she would carefully put all the jokes back in. It was a war of attrition. I was never going to resign because, although the money was nothing much, I really needed it. Richard was never going to sack me because that's not his way. We avoided each other at social events.

In 2014, though, there was a mighty hoo-hah at the *Oldie* as Richard had fallen out with James Pembroke, by now proprietor of the magazine. Richard resigned in a fury, thinking he was irreplaceable, and not realising until it was too late that he had made a grave strategic error. He and his wife sent around emails to all the contributors asking them to resign in sympathy. Several did, but I thought, sod that for a game of soldiers. Loyalty works both ways. You show me some and I might show some to you in return. I decided to stay. James was delighted and gave me a small pay rise. The new editor was Alexander Chancellor, who was actually an old friend of Richard's, so that must have gone down well in the Ingrams household. Alexander seemed to like my work, so I continued as before.

In 2017, though, Alexander went into hospital for what appeared to be a minor complaint and rather unfortunately died. Contributors to the *Oldie* died all the time, for obvious demographic reasons, but editors tended to stay alive for ever. James replaced him with a young pup named Harry Mount, son of Ferdinand, who wasn't even fifty yet but was reassuringly bald and had preternaturally shiny shoes. We all thought that Harry would be James's creature, easily manipulated by the old rogue, who would surely be stroking a white cat as he adjusted his monocle. But not a bit of it. Harry made many more changes than Alexander had. He shifted the tone, making the magazine more serious and much more posh. Being neither of those things, I began to feel vulnerable. I may talk a good game, but I went to a minor public school and I am very much not one of the Worcestershire Berkmanns. Harry also wanted me to shift my working practice and review only films that hadn't come out yet, which I argued would make my column exactly like everybody else's. That, of course, was what he wanted. Unlike Richard and Alexander, who were both contrarians to a fault, Harry is deeply conventional, straight-down-the-line *Daily Telegraph*. He was also a micro-manager, constantly telling me what to do and which films to see, which I can't bear. For several months he made my life a misery, until in despair I chucked it all in. 'You can't resign a column!' said everyone. I just have done, I replied.

But here's a thing. Six months after I resigned the column, I realised that in the interim I hadn't been to see a single film. Harry, whether he realised it or not, had been right. The column had run out of steam, and the last person to see this had been the person writing it. The next time I saw Harry, I greeted him as an old friend and thanked him for having done me a favour. He looked as bemused and posh as ever, and looked down with his customary horror at my less than preternaturally shiny shoes.

10

Work Life

'Tip 2: take inspiration from the greats, but don't compare yourself to them. Compare yourself to the mediocre men who flourish everywhere.'

Suzanne Moore's tips for female writers

I am a morning person. I write in the mornings, every morning, seven days a week. Afternoons are for reading and sleep. Evening is for fun. (But not too much fun. There's work to do tomorrow morning.)

Realising you work best in the morning (or whenever) is something that happens only gradually, and in my case over about twenty years. I was talking to another writer friend about this, Russell, who writes (but does not draw) a daily cartoon strip. He reckoned he had four productive creative hours a day, and I think I do too. If I have a real surge and do, say, seven or eight hours of serious head-work in a single twenty-four-hour period, the following morning I wake up dim and useless. Over time I believe most people's hours of genuine effectiveness average out at about four a day. Russell knows bankers who are in work at 7 a.m. and don't leave before 10 p.m., but he says they think they have four good hours a day as well. The rest of the time is used up by meetings, lunch, gossip and furiously appearing to work while actually day-dreaming. One fellow I heard about has an even more useful skill, the ability to sleep for short periods with his eyes open. Forget being good at his job: this is what makes him envied by all his co-workers and given endless pay rises by his seniors.

My 'alpha time' starts when I wake up, usually about eight, and goes on until about half past twelve. I then have a little beta time before plunging head-first into omega time. Any time spent work-ing during omega time is a waste of time. You might as well go to sleep, and as I get older I find there is little choice in the matter. You lie on the bed, you open a book and forty-five minutes later you wake up. Daytime naps, it turns out, have almost no downside. They are good for you spiritually, physically, mentally. We are pro-grammed to resist them not by our bodies, but by our bosses, who want us working all hours until we keel over at our desks. Those bosses have themselves asked not to be disturbed between the hours of three and four because they are reading important reports, horizontally, with a pillow under their heads. What a coincidence that they all have sofas in their offices. What a coincidence that their exhausted underlings do not.

If you have a daytime nap, according to recent research, you will be 20 per cent more effective at your work when you wake up. That may not sound like much, but it could be the difference between doing a little light filing and crawling along the carpet on all fours begging for a cup of tea. Daytime naps do not affect your night's sleep, and if regularly indulged in, may actually enhance it, because people who battle through the tired hours often get overtired in the evening and then can't get to sleep at all. I suspect, though I have no proof of this, that afternoon kipping makes you live longer as well, because it reduces your stress levels to those of the average two-toed sloth, and as we all know, stress kills, in many different ways. I am hoping this is the case, because if it is, I have had so many naps over the years I should live to 120.

I said that daytime napping has *almost* no downsides, but it can make collaboration difficult. When I was working on comedy stuff with Harry Thompson, we quickly found that our working days didn't match at all. I was best in the morning but Harry could not function or even speak before lunchtime. He was best in the afternoon when I was asleep. So we usually worked in the evenings, when we both weren't bad. In the end, this may have contributed to the dismal failure of almost all our collaborations, although I also think that failure begets failure, especially in a collaboration. The more your work is rejected, the worse it gets. This certainly applied to us.

Richard, my co-writer on the doomed film script, was a different type altogether. As a film director, and a driven man who rarely blinked, he could work long hours without the smallest diminution in intensity. Whereas after lunch I was toast. I think he thought I was doing it on purpose to annoy him. He was staring at the computer trying to resolve the problem in scene 46 – an impossible task because the problem was that the scene wasn't any good – while I was lying on the sofa in his office, positioning my head so that he couldn't see that my eyes were closed. I couldn't deceive him, though, after the snores started.

(Years after we had given up trying to write with each other, Harry rang up. He had sold an idea for a scabrous, satirical animated series and they needed the scripts in a hurry. His usual co-writer was fitfully employed on something else, so Harry wondered if I might be free for a few afternoon sessions writing with him. He already had all his ideas mapped out, so the sketches just needed to be written. I probably only spent four or five afternoons working with him, but they were four or five of the most joyous afternoons of my career. For once in my life I was just a writer for hire. We wrote huge quantities of material, every last bit of it was used, I was well paid, and the series turned into *Monkey Dust*, which I still think was the best work Harry ever did.)

Here's a typical writer's day, mapped out hour after hour. Snack breaks are not included.

7.20 Wake up, think I really should get up and get on with some work. Turn over and go back to sleep.

8.10 Finally wake up, as hungry cat is sitting on my head. Get up, grumbling, snuffling and scratching.

8.12 First look in the mirror of the day. I am either an unusually well-preserved eighty-five-year-old or a seventy-five-year-old who has known great suffering.

8.13 Put kettle on, feed cat, get the *Guardian* from the doorstep.

8.18 TEA. VATS OF IT.

8.30 The *Guardian* is full of misery. Ready to start work.

8.30–10.00 The best hours of the day. A problem you couldn't solve in an hour the previous evening will take five minutes first thing in the morning. I am lucky, also, in that my powers of concentration are either naturally strong or have grown in strength over the years. Whatever else is going on in the flat – Mum! Where are my socks? – I'm in my bubble and nothing can disturb me.

10.00 A vague presentiment suggests that something is wrong. What could it be? A loud rumble from my stomach tells me I haven't eaten yet. Eat yogurt. Back to work.

10.01–12.30 Mind still working well but slightly less well than in the first hour and a half. It could be time for the second breakfast (bowl of muesli) or a creative mid-morning bath. In the bath I wash all my bits in the usual order while constructing the next couple of sentences in my head. If I can wash myself without the slightest memory afterwards of having done so, the brain is working at full capacity.

Outside the bath, it's also important to pause every half hour or so to walk pointlessly around the flat, do some washing-up or make some more tea. Facebook and emails are useful distractions.* When I used to work on the script with Richard, he would stare for hour after hour at the computer screen, willing the brilliant idea to appear there in front of him. It doesn't work like that for me. I usually have to tease a brilliant idea out of the undergrowth. Then grab it with both hands and not let it go.

12.30–1.00 Ideas are becoming ever harder to grasp and the slippery little bastards are getting away. Unless you have a heavy deadline, this is the time to stop. Everything else you write today will almost certainly be unusable.

1.00–4.00 Lunch, book, sleep.

4.00 Time for tea again. I allow myself three cups in the morning and two in the afternoon, for otherwise I become lighter than air and start walking across the ceiling.

4.15–6.30 Beta time for admin, filing, reading, probably more washing-up.

6.30 (if not going out on the town whooping it up) Walk around the streets near my home, letting my mind wander. This is remarkably useful for working out what you're going to do tomorrow and thinking about problems you often didn't know you had.

This sounds a pretty easy life and I could now pretend how complex and demanding and exhausting it all is, how I toil thanklessly at the wordface in order to provide small bowls of gruel for my ever huger and greedier family, who are always asking for cheques for things, which I write with a shaky hand and a tear in my eye. Well, the latter part is actually true, but the rest of it is great. As I mentioned earlier, writers all complain incessantly about their lives, but let's be honest: we don't need to go to an office, we never have to have meetings, we can make sure we only travel on public transport outside rush hour, and occasionally we can go

---

* The former described by Nicholas Lezard as 'the water-cooler of the internet where writers gather to piss away the time, especially when deadlines loom'.

for long boozy lunches with our friends. It's a life a little low on excitement – the biggest thrill I have had in ages was when I found a Cadbury's Double Decker I had hidden in the sock drawer and completely forgotten about – but excitement is overrated. In some ways the person I feel closest to in this household is the cat, who has only three interests in life, food, more food and finding the warmest place in the flat where he can lie down and go to sleep.

There's also the question of energy, which is a horribly random variable. I interviewed a professor the other day, who writes books and broadcasts regularly and does research and teaches postgraduates and sits on committees, and I said, how do you do it all? I don't stop, he said, I love it. He doesn't know why, but he has boundless energy, and can put in a really intense sixteen-hour day without blinking. If I put in a really intense sixteen-hour day, I would have to take to my bed for a week. But one of the many benefits of age is that you learn how to marshal what energy you have and make the most of it. By the standards of some people I have little energy, but my god do I use every last scrap of it.

I have written before about the psychological phenomenon of flow, and it continues to fascinate me. Flow is when you become so engrossed in something that time seems to move more quickly. In my case it's roughly twice as quickly. If I'm running a bath, I have to go down to the bathroom and check it when I think it would be half run, and it's already full. I play music while I work, and a CD seems to last half as long as it should last. If there is a secret to human happiness, it may be flow. Funnily enough, I only get it now when I'm writing something long form, like a book. Journalism used to be a source of flow and it isn't any more. Much journalism, as I get older, seems to be more a source of anxiety, because I'm not as good with deadlines I used to be. I never miss one, but I worry more about missing one, which sucks the pleasure out of writing like a huge comedy syringe. But writing this book has been so enjoyable that I have had flow almost every day. I have the same worries as usual, but during this period I have been a nicer person than I usually am. I stroke the cat rather than kick it. I merely shout at the children rather than beat them remorselessly with sticks. I am calmer and kinder, and it's all down to flow.

What's missing from this rosy, optimistic picture? The days of failure, of course. This whole portrait of work life operates on the assumption that the words are pouring out, that the brain is functioning and that the teabags haven't run out. There are other kinds of days too, the days in which nothing is happening, in which the brain is replaced by a large grey sponge, when you simply can't write for toffee. It's funny how some days you can be fluent and witty and to the point, and other days you simply cannot write at all. This is no exaggeration. Your every sentence clunks. Your thoughts are dull and third hand. To all intents and purposes, you have temporarily ceased to be a writer.

When I was younger and in more of a hurry than I am now, this was a big worry. If you have a deadline of 3 p.m. for a TV review, you *have* to have written 610 adequate words by 3 p.m. Some days I could barely write my name. In those circumstances you simply have to battle through and produce something. It may take five times as long to produce something barely half as good as your normal stuff, but there isn't another option.

These days I don't have such ferocious deadlines, and accordingly I like to produce my copy as early as possible, sometimes even a day or two before it has to be filed. This means that a dead day can simply be written off, forgotten about. I might just read a book instead, or go and buy some Maltesers. Try again tomorrow, when with luck the stars will align and I'll be a writer again.

The one question putative writers all ask writers is, do you get writer's block? Funny, really. You don't ask a hairdresser if he gets hairdresser's block and some days can't cut hair to save his life. Yet writers get asked this all the time, probably because the people asking the question think they could probably have been great writers if they hadn't suffered from writer's block for 365 days in the past year. Leo Tolstoy, grand panjandrum of bearded Russian writers, once said that professional writers are people who find it hard to write. Somehow you know that it was snowing when he said this, and the heating had failed. But Tolstoy also advised writers not to write at all unless they felt it was absolutely necessary, and never with an eye to publication. This may be my cynical twenty-first-century view, but I'm sure he was just trying to discourage the competition. Tolstoy, who only ever wrote for money like all sensible people, had his rules for life, which included:

- Wake at five o'clock.
- Go to bed no later than ten o'clock.
- Two hours permissible for sleeping during the day.
- Eat moderately.
- Avoid sweet foods.
- Walk for an hour a day.
- Disregard all public opinion not based on reason.
- Disallow flights of imagination unless necessary.
- Help those less fortunate.
- Visit a brothel only twice a month.

All excellent suggestions. It's probably worth mentioning here that Tolstoy fathered fourteen children.

So I would never admit to writer's block, and the truth is that, the odd day aside, I rarely suffer from it. Even so, I sit at the computer *every morning of my life* and wonder whether this won't be the day when it all stops, when my career comes to an end. And somehow, from somewhere, the first sentence comes. It might not be any good. But once you've got something on the page, you can do something with it. And every time I finish a piece I feel utter relief and gratitude, even surprise, that the end didn't come today.

Maybe it'll come tomorrow, but I'm not going to worry about it until then.

The truth is, everyone's different. What works for me won't necessarily work for you, or the sex-crazed elderly Russian novelist living down the road. All that matters, in the end, is that you produce the words on time, without complaint, and ideally in the right order.

11

Disraeli's Hairstyle

'A freelance writer is a man who is paid per piece or per word or perhaps.'

Robert Benchley

There is, and always has been, something a little strange about my connection to the *Daily Mail*. I don't share its politics, or much of its worldview, and I've had some terrible scrapes there, which for other people might have been career-ending. Back in the early days, when I was still the paper's pop critic, David English had a ridiculous idea, which was that anyone could be a rock star, anyone at all. You didn't need talent, you didn't need to be able to sing, or write songs, or do anything other than look good in a suit. To prove this (essentially facile) theory, he decided that I, young and symmetric of face, could be turned into a rock star with a little bit of grooming and some money splashed about. (The *Mail* may not always have the best ideas, but money is never a problem.) First, I was taken to Covent Garden and dressed in the latest fashionable clobber, which to my surprise I looked quite good in. The photos, which will surely be unearthed as blackmail material should I ever attain sufficient fame, did make me look gayer than George Michael, but perhaps fortunately I wasn't allowed to keep any of the clothes, which would have been completely out of fashion twenty-seven minutes later. After the photo shoot, I was whisked off to a recording studio in west London to record a single, the music of which had been bought off the shelf and, this being around 1991, sounded a bit like Kylie Minogue's early hits, as everything did then. This was where the wheels fell off. Having been essentially ordered to do this, I had acceded to everyone's requests so far, and my minder for the project was an old bruiser called Rod Gilchrist, who was David English's right-hand man and known and feared throughout the paper as his enforcer. But when we got into the studio, it was discovered that not only could I not sing technically, I couldn't sing physically either. Standing in front of that microphone, failing to sing for what seemed like a whole afternoon, was one of the most humiliating experiences of my young life, and I remember sitting in the studio café afterwards, weeping with frustration, anger and despair. I remember saying, I don't remember whether this means the end of my career at the *Mail*, I can't do this and I'm not doing this. I also remember, bizarrely, meeting Shakin' Stevens for the first and only time, in that same café. He was literally rigid with fear at the thought of all these tabloid journalists prowling around in that vaguely threatening way they all have. After several hours of this, I was allowed to go home and forget all about it, and some junior reporter (female) was given the task instead. Tens of thousands of pounds were spent, the single was an abject failure, the piece the poor girl had to write afterwards was dismal and by the following day the whole idea had been forgotten about by everyone.

Well, by everyone except Rod Gilchrist, who I still bump into from time to time. I'm not sure he had seen anyone cry before, especially not a thirty-year-old *Daily Mail* columnist, and he thought this so patently ridiculous that he would remind me of it every time I saw him. In later years, after retiring from the *Mail*, he regularly used to try to sell a story to newspapers about the whole dismal sequence of events, but fortunately no one ever bought it. In fact, this could be the first time the tale has ever been told in print.

A few months later I was appointed deputy TV critic.

Another job I occasionally had in the early 1990s was to write features for the paper, or what were variously called 'page eights' or 'page nines', depending whether the piece was printed on page eight or page nine, as you may have worked out. Also known as 'op eds' (for 'opposite the editorial page'), these ranting and raging opinion pieces were rechristened 'Why Oh Whys' by *Private Eye*, which summed them up perfectly. You'd be rung up at around midday, after conference, and asked to write a piece on *EastEnders*, or *Star Trek*, or something else in the news that day that you were supposed to know about. The fee for these pieces was magical: £800 at the very least, and sometimes climbing to £1200, which is very much worth three or four hours' work, however uncongenial that work may turn out to be. You had to file between 900 and 1100 words at four, and then wait to see what happened. If the features department were on the phone every fifteen minutes demanding rewrites, that was a good sign, as it meant that your piece might be used. The *Mail* had so much money in those days that they would regularly commission four or five different pieces for the same page, lay them out, show them to the editor of the day and let him choose which one he preferred. The others would just be abandoned, although they always paid a generous kill fee. It quickly became apparent that it was much easier and better for one's mental health to write for the kill fee. The problem was that, in order to please the editor and get your piece in the paper, you had to write such arrant drivel that your friends would be teasing you about it for months. My friend David Thomas, who had edited *Punch*, had a rare ability to write these terrible articles, and did at least one a week for several years. It earned him a fortune, but killed his newspaper career elsewhere like a guillotine.

When I decamped for the *Sunday Express* in 1996, the requests to write these pieces had already, thankfully, dried up, but a few years later the features department started calling me again and once or twice, when enormous bills loomed, I'm afraid I succumbed. By now I was less young and less foolish and needed several baths to rid me of the taint. One day the features editor rang me up and said, was I free that day?

Yes, I said.

We'd like you to do a hatchet job on Michael Parkinson, he said.

I thought for a moment and said, no, I don't think so.

Really? said the features editor, shocked to his core. Why?

Because I don't dislike Michael Parkinson, and I don't want to do it.

They never called again.

After a while, you just have to accept that what will be will be. When I think of all the effort I put in to trying to get into the *Guardian*, with no success at all, I could weep. They probably think I'm as right wing as David Thomas. But there always seemed to be a way back into the *Mail*. In late 2003 the women who run the books pages had heard that I did the odd quiz, and would I like to write a literary quiz for their pages over Christmas? I would indeed. They liked it, and it became an annual gig. On the third or fourth of my literary quizzes, I came up with an idea for a round that required me to go into the office for an afternoon and read their cuttings files. And so I met the *Daily Mail* Books Women.

I am still writing a literary quiz for them every year and I still go in for an afternoon in early December to research the same round, but to be honest I'd find a way of going in even if there was no research to do. The Books Women, currently Sandra Parsons, Susie Dowdall and Sally Morris, are a hoot. They don't just put together their three or four pages of reviews every Friday, they also arrange the book serialisations, which can be amazingly stressful, because they often have to move fast (to secure the books the editor favours) and everything can go badly wrong at great speed. They must also keep on the right side of publishing PRs, butter up authors and editors and, possibly most arduously of all, talk down some of their reviewers, one or two of whom are barking mad. After I got to know the Books Women, I too joined the ranks of their reviewers. It's not incredibly regular work – sometimes you're in fashion, and then suddenly you're out of fashion and they don't call you for months – but it is satisfying and well paid, a rare and beautiful combination.

The Books Women occupy a small, book-packed office slightly out of the run of things, although people do drop in to share the time of day. Considering how much time they spend together, they do seem to get on very well, sharing a sense of humour so mordant you'd expect it to drip blood. But I think they're under such pressure, as everyone always has been at the *Mail*, that if they didn't get on, they'd go bonkers. Fortunately, they are also eminently distractible. The last time I went in, the subject of the conversation turned to the Hollywood actor and screenwriter Billy Bob Thornton, and I told them that Billy Bob Thornton has a morbid fear of Disraeli's hairstyle.

No, said Sandra, surely not.

Yes, said I, and he has a series of utterly bizarre phobias you'd never expect. He's certainly terrified of some sort of furniture, and I can't remember the rest.

Well, that was it for Sandra, who interrupted whatever else she was doing to investigate Billy Bob Thornton's irrational fears on the internet. Every so often there'd be a cry of astonishment as she unearthed another one.*

Like the rest of the paper, the *Daily Mail* books pages have a particular tone that is easy to identify and hard to define. All the big reviews (which range from six hundred words to twelve hundred) are of non-fiction books, and almost all of them are positive. Occasionally I am sent a book that is so awful I have to ring up the Books Women and give them the bad news. They always say, poor you, just forget it, we'll get you something else. They're not interested in shitting on the incompetent, the poorly written, the pompous or the dull, because they see their job as leading people in the direction of books that are genuinely worth reading. Or as Susie once said, 'We only have four pages, so it's always felt a bit of a waste to use our treasured space on duds.' As a result, the *Daily Mail* books pages are an oasis of kindness in a newspaper that has been known to be stridently negative about pretty much everything else.

Many journalists, possibly even most journalists, would say that it's far easier to be negative in your writing than it is to be positive. Slagging things off is much more fun, even if it's Michael Parkinson. And maybe it is when you're young, buoyed up by confidence and ego, not particularly concerned by the deleterious effects your words may have on their victims. I was quite a fearless writer in my thirties: I didn't mind who I upset. As I have aged, that seems to have changed. Writing sneery book reviews for *Private Eye* has become more difficult; writing positive ones for the *Daily Mail* has become easier. This may just be me, of course. Having written a few books myself, I know how hard it is to write even a really bad book, and much of the time it just seems cruel to let the world know how bad it

---

* He has aviophobia (fear of flying), and as well as his fear of Disraeli's hairstyle (because of a film he saw as a child), he is morbidly terrified of antiques (particularly the idea of sleeping or eating near furniture made before 1950) and of bright colours, particularly orange food.

is, especially if the author is not widely known. Of course this does not apply to the books of the famous, the arrogant and the mentally ill, which is why I continue to rip apart the memoirs of celebrities in the *Eye* with a murderous glint in my eye.

That said, my old friend David (D. J.) Taylor thinks that book reviewers are too soft on too many books these days, and that there isn't as much room in newspapers' book pages as there used to be for righteous indignation. He may be right. We have all read the latest novel everyone is talking about, that is lathered with critical praise, that turns out to be so frustratingly awful you want to chuck it out of the window. So for a book reviewer, there are some tricky balances you have to maintain: be positive but not bland; or be negative but not smug. Blandness is a perennial enemy, especially if the reviewer is inadequate, or simply not engaged by the book. But a book review isn't just telling you how good or bad a book is: it has to be an entertainment in itself. You are writing for four distinct groups of people: your editors (the most important of all); the book's writer and publisher, for whom this may represent several years' work; the readers who might be tempted to buy the book (so don't overpraise); and the readers who will never buy the book but just want to be amused for three minutes or so. What none of them need is what they often get: a sixth-form essay full of ill-formed judgements that the book's writer, who is a sensitive soul, will neither forgive nor forget.

(For one of my earlier books I got a paragraph-long mini-review in one paper, complaining that the book wasn't the one the reviewer wanted to read on the subject. It was too jokey, not serious enough. This was a total failure on the part of the reviewer. It was his job to review the book he had been given, not the one he wanted it to be. If you want it that much, I wanted to tell him, write the fucking thing yourself.*)

---

* This was twenty years ago. It still rankles.

Again, here are a couple of excerpts as tasters. This is the start of my review of a memoir of the comedian Linda Smith:

> When the comedian Linda Smith died of ovarian cancer last year at the desperately early age of forty-eight, an awful lot of people who had never met her felt genuine grief. When most celebrities die, you think, 'Oh well, never mind,' and in one or two cases you might be tempted to put out the flags and bunting. But Linda Smith! We hadn't even known she was ill! It seemed so unfair that such a singular talent should be silenced in this cruel and random way, and it still does. Radio 4, and by extension the internal lives of millions, are poorer for her absence.
>
> Warren Lakin was her partner, sounding-board, driver and amanuensis for twenty-three years ... He is particularly good on her early years. Linda Smith grew up in Erith in south-east London, 'a place so grim and miserable and meaningless and depressing, it's not actually twinned with anywhere, but it does have a suicide pact with Dagenham'. She used a lot of autobiographical material in her act, which must have made researching this book rather easier, but Lakin has been assiduous in filling the gaps. 'Her early health record mentions she had a bad cold at thirteen months, stating that it was "caused by talking".' Aged six or seven, Linda did everything she could to stop her older sister getting married. 'The vicar came round to check where we lived,' says her sister. 'He knocked at the door and said, "Are Barbara and Terry here?" Linda said, "No, nobody of that name here." And slammed the door.'

It's always important, when writing book reviews, to quote liberally from the book. This gives your reader a useful sense of what it might be like to read it, while also filling in valuable space that would otherwise be occupied by words you would have to write yourself.

Duncan Bannatyne once wrote a book called *How to Be Smart with Your Time*. It was very nearly worth reading all the way to the end.

> Bannatyne is of course the perpetually disbelieving one on *Dragons' Den*, a man who has made £320 million out of his various business activities and, more importantly, kept it. Like all entrepreneurs he is a driven man, propelled initially, we learn, by the early death of his sister. 'This might look like a book about time management, but it's really about fulfilling your dreams and living a life without regret.' To which end he invites you to answer two fundamental questions:
>
> 1. What are you doing with your life?
> 2. What are you doing today?
>
> To be smart with your time, he says, you need to balance long-term goals with short-term needs. Along the way there are three disciplines we must master. First, compromise. Perfectionism takes too much time, says Bannatyne. Second best is usually good enough. Next, focus. Turn off your phone, turn down some invitations, and concentrate. Last of all, decision-making. The sooner you can make your mind up about one thing, the quicker you can move on to the next. 'Being indecisive squanders time and opportunity and is the enemy of progress.' After a couple of hours reading this book, you'll even eat a biscuit with new vigour and determination.

I wrote this review at great speed as a tribute to Bannatyne's extraordinary sagacity.

Reading through these reviews again, I realised that, while

books last for ever, book reviewing is a strictly ephemeral art. The only resonance a review ever has is when the paperback comes out a year later and you look through it in a bookshop to see whether your review has been quoted. ('A work of shimmering genius' – *Daily Mail*. This isn't a patch on 'A work of shimmering genius' – Marcus Berkmann, *Daily Mail*.)

And unlike TV and film reviewing, where silk purses are constantly made of sow's ears, the quality of the review depends not just on the quality of the reviewer, but the quality of the book. The most difficult job in the world is to write a decent piece about a book you don't care about. I once did a Lady Antonia Fraser history book which I found so boring I wanted to scream. The review took forever to write and wasn't any good at all.

It's also remarkable how few of the books I review stay on my shelves for long. This may be because my shelves are already jam-packed with books I read for pleasure. Review copies, however much I enjoyed them, tend to end up in Oxfam. But while long-term TV and film reviewing effectively obliterated my long-term enthusiasm for TV and films, book reviewing hasn't done the same to books. It probably helps that I only review, and write, non-fiction, while I read fiction for fun. But a pile of books coming through the post in an oversized Jiffy bag still gives me a jolt of excitement, and not just because of the money I'm about to earn. The same is true of all the book reviewers I know. You can never have too many books, because even far too many is never quite enough.

12

Peripheries

'Writers don't need love: all they require is money.'

John Osborne

Technology

Every writer needs his computer. Nowadays it's more than likely to be a laptop, small and compact, and taking up so much less room than the behemoths of technology used to, with their vast screens, mighty fans, infinite number of accessories and more leads than you can find in an electrical supply shop. In the days when all writers' offices looked like the bridge of the USS *Enterprise*, our friends often jumped to the conclusion that we were terribly au fait with technology, that we knew which plug went into where and why, and that we knew which button to press to print something out, which would, when pressed, actually print something out. The fools.

As it happens, almost all writers hate and despise their laptops, and even more, hate and despise the people who programmed them. The problem with computers is that they are designed by nerds, who have no more understanding of how the non-nerdish mind works than they are likely to have sex with anyone, ever. (The two may be connected.) Even on the Apple Macintosh, a computer designed to be user-friendly above all else, there are ways of doing things that make no sense at all, other than to the person who programmed them. I have long had a theory that Apple's titanic profits and bulbous share price have more to do with the damage inflicted on their products by generations of furious writers who cannot operate them and don't want to be told 'how easy' it is, than by any sniff of corporate excellence. You lose your temper, you throw your computer out of the window, you have to go and buy another one. Ker-ching! for the late Steve Jobs, Tim Cook and all the dead-eyed number-crunchers toiling in the company's super-white dust-free brain-factories all around the world.

Why? Because nerds are almost exactly the opposite of us. If you're mostly analytical and methodical in your thinking, you are said to be left-brained. If you tend to be more creative and artistic, you are said to be right-brained. It's said that when the left side and the right side of the brain started to talk to each other, that's when human beings formed language, invented agriculture and became the dominant species on Earth. Quite a few millennia later, however, the left side of nerds' brains and the right side of writers' brains are definitely not talking to each other. All you have to do to prove this is call a computer helpline with your astonishingly trivial problem. After you have hung on the phone for twenty minutes in a queue, you finally reach the on-duty nerd, who is already eating his forty-third packet of crisps this morning. You tell him what's wrong and – this is absolutely guaranteed – the nerd will utter a sigh of such length and such utter contempt that it's all you can do not to slam the phone down on him. How can you not know this? is his unspoken rejoinder. Because I'm a successful writer and you are an idiot wearing a Kings of Leon T-shirt, is yours. Some nerds, who know how to speak creative, will be able to guide you through the steps needed to solve your problem, most of them hopelessly counter-intuitive. Other, less gifted nerds will speak to you in what might as well be a foreign language. These are people who know how things work, and they care that they know. You do not know, and you do not care. This will never be a meeting of minds.

On Facebook I know a lot of writers who are constantly asking each other about their computer problems because they can't spare the time or the blood vessels in their brain to ring a computer helpline. I feel their pain, although obviously at the same time I am feeling my own, because my printer is making funny squealing noises, the piece I wrote yesterday has vanished, the internet is slower than a ninety-six-year-old on a Zimmer frame and my email address is only receiving spam from Ukrainian transgender porn sites. I might take to my bed later, and start writing on parchment with a quill pen.

Twitter

I have a friend who tweets a lot. And I mean a lot. Sometimes fifteen, occasionally twenty, even twenty-five tweets emerge from his keyboard *every day*. He tweets when he has a cup of coffee. He tweets when he can't decide whether or not to have a second cup of coffee. I've heard that his next book is nearly a year late.

There are many distractions open to the procrastinating writer. I walk around the flat, watch some cricket on the telly, ring my friends. I look at Facebook half a dozen times a day, scrolling down through all the posts people already had up the last time I looked. But the most ruthlessly efficient timewaster of them all has to be Twitter. It eats the hours and its appetite is never sated. It also eats the soul. You get into some pointless political argument with someone you don't know and will never meet and WHOOSH! two hours have gone.

Unfortunately, publishers of books and editors of newspapers are all obsessed with Twitter. If I had a pound coin for every time I have been told I *needed* to be on Twitter, I'd be so weighed down by metal I'd be struggling to walk down the stairs. Most articles you read in newspapers feature the writer's Twitter address prominently displayed, so if you think they're talking rubbish, you can contact them directly and threaten to cut off their balls and shove them straight up their arse. Or, if they're women, rape them and kill them and bury them in soft peat. There seems to be little room for civilised discourse on Twitter, where disagreement of even the mildest sort predicates violence and, possibly, long prison sentences. Why bother? Why do any of it? Because you need to be in touch with your public, they tell me. One of the benefits of obscurity, I say, is that I don't actually have a public. I just have a private, and I'm determined to keep it that way.

Writers, though, often have complex personalities – which is to say, far too complex for something as simplistic as Twitter. I know introverts who love showing off; egomaniacs with sensitive skins; men (especially) who like to express strong opinions while not necessarily having to hear other people's even stronger opinions expressed to them in return. The point is, writers all have something to say but not necessarily all the correct psychological equipment for saying it. None of this matters on Twitter. All the maddest people in the world, or at least all those not currently locked up in institutions for the criminally insane, are currently tweeting something so pointless, foolish and obviously wrong that they should count themselves lucky still to have their freedom. Let them get on with it! Have a bath! Empty your mind!

The boozy lunch

It's assumed by many people who have proper jobs that writers are, in the main, ne'er-do-wells and layabouts who love nothing more than to go out for a long boozy lunch that lasts well into the evening and sees them rolling home, half-cut, to fall asleep in front of the telly and snore like a bison. As it happens, this is true. While we are all extremely diligent and work at our craft until we have nothing more to give, everyone needs a little downtime. I myself need as much as I can get, and lunch is merely the start of it.

Keith Waterhouse, the columnist and playwright who for the last twenty-five years of his life had a very large red nose, used to work every morning and sign off at lunchtime, rather as I do. I spend most afternoons either sleeping or reading or doing dreary admin, whereas Keith, who had some style, took out a clean glass and opened a bottle of champagne. (I never met him, which was my loss.) I wouldn't say that all writers are drinkers, because some are manifestly not, even the ones I know. But those who do like a drop like it a lot, and they need company. It turns out that I'm only a phone call away.

There are two sorts of boozy lunch we need to consider here, the informal and the formal. The informal lunch is one that usually starts innocently. One friend calls another, suggests meeting for lunch, the other says yes. Both have it in mind just to go to a pub or a restaurant, eat their food, chew the fat, depart with a manly handshake – or a womanly mwah! – and go home and drink tea. And indeed, many lunches proceed in this harmless, pleasantly sociable manner. But then there are one or two that don't . . .

I think that the decisive factor here is number of personnel. If there are just two of you, you can easily keep things under control. Three is more perilous, but once you reach five or six you really are asking for trouble. And if they are all writers – which means they almost certainly have nothing more important to do that afternoon – you might as well take along your own stomach pump and be done with it.

Some writers are, of course, notorious drunks and they are probably to be avoided, unless you like notorious drunks, of course. The few serious piss-artists I know may all be more or less functional alcoholics, but at least you know that lunch with them isn't going to end at half past two, or necessarily in the same city where you started. Shouldn't we have a higher loyalty to our sad drunken friends that prevents us from contributing to and collaborating with this catastrophic taste for self-destruction? Probably, but if it wasn't with us it would be with someone else, and why should they have all the fun?

Formal boozy lunches are rarer and more cherishable, and often have the enormous advantage of being free. I only go to a couple these days: the Oldie of the Year awards lunch at Simpson's in the Strand in January or February, and the occasional *Private Eye* lunch. The Oldie of the Year lunch has been running for twenty years and I have been to nearly all of them. As well as the magazine's contributors, sponsors and supporters, famous not-terribly-young people are also invited, so you could find yourself (as I have) sitting opposite Barry Norman, the cricket-loving film critic (so we had a lot to talk about), or, another year, between Jenni Murray, formerly of *Woman's Hour*, and Kate Adie, the intrepid foreign correspondent. I quite like sitting next to celebs, as they always have something unusual and unexpected to say. Bill Nighy once told me about his passion for late 1970s funk music, which he loved so much he thought he had heard all of it. There wasn't any left. I knew little about late 1970s funk music, but I totally understood his enthusiasm. Famous people never want to talk about their work. Get them onto any other subject, and off they'll go.

Private Eye lunches are legendary, not for their alcoholic intake but for the quality and variety of the guests. I go to two or three a year and have sat next to some fascinating people, and one or two monumental bores, and almost every variety of humanity in between. Most *Eye* lunches end at a normal time, somewhere north of four o'clock, with the diligent returning to their offices to 'do more work' (fall asleep at their desks). Just occasionally, though, the last few hangers-on get a second wind, and I have been to one or two lunches where darkness has fallen before people staggered off. Everyone gets a bit light-headed, as though they are doing something naughty and are waiting to be told off.

It's like staying in the pub for the whole afternoon. When you arrive, it's busy with fellow lunchers. But gradually they disappear, back to their offices, and then the pub is almost deserted. Tumbleweed blows through the lounge bar and the landlord turns up the volume on Sky Sports. Then, at about five o'clock, the first and thirstiest of the post-work crowd come through the door. By half past six the pub is full again, and you're still there, sitting in the same seats with the same people, talking the same rubbish you were talking six hours earlier. If there is a higher state of grace than this, I have yet to encounter it.

Driving

The first writer I was aware of who couldn't, or wouldn't, drive was Kingsley Amis, who may have been able to but chose not to because it would interfere with his drinking. Minicabs feature prominently in his later novels.

I am not in Kingsley's class as a gargler, but I can't drive either. Not that this was ever the intention. Other than three years at university, I have lived all my life in London, where public transport is plentiful and cheap. Learning to drive was easy to put off. In my twenties, I was far too impoverished even to consider buying a car. Then, for several years, I was too busy, and then, suddenly, I was forty and it was now or never. I have known a few writers who have learned to drive at forty, compelled to do so by furious spouses, but my own furious spouse had said, when we started going out, that she was a control freak who preferred driving and made an unusually poor and demanding passenger, and I believed her. Years later I reminded her of this and she denied having ever said it, having herself become even more furious because of all the driving she had had to do. But by then it really was too late. My nerve had gone, and if I had learned to drive at fifty or fifty-one, I would have done well to reach fifty-two. By then it has to be a muscle memory if you are not to be a menace on the roads.

The extraordinary thing is how many other writers I have encountered who either can't drive, or prefer not to drive, or learned late to mollify partners. Why is this? Amongst the rest of the population, not being able to drive a car is a sign of serious eccentricity. In writers, it's verging on normal. I have one or two theories about this, but few conclusions.

One is spatial awareness. Mine is terrible. I am appallingly clumsy and I am constantly bumping into things that shouldn't be there. If I were a driver, I fear I should be constantly bumping into things that shouldn't be there, like trees or pantechnicons. I know other writers who have the same problem, who can't see a staircase without falling down it. But which comes first, the chicken or the egg? Do people with poor spatial awareness become writers, because it's the only job they can do without killing themselves? Or do writers achieve poor spatial awareness, because they are in their heads all the time thinking about the next sentence, and not concentrating on the cup of tea they're about to drop?

Another possible reason is walking. Show me a writer who doesn't go walking all the time, and you'll show me a writer who doesn't do much writing either. Walking is the only form of exercise that frees up your mind to think of more important things, and there's nothing more important than your work. Driving, according to friends of mine who know, also frees up your mind, but only if you have been doing it so long you can do it without thinking about it. I doubt this is a mental state that is known to many writers.

I also wonder whether some writers do not drive because there's nowhere in particular they want to go. The most dedicated driver I have ever known (not a writer) was a restless soul, constantly ending relationships, starting new ones, moving house, moving city, and bombing up the nearest motorway at 100 mph whenever he felt angry or frustrated. Whereas most writers are never happier than when sitting in front of their computer keyboard, trying to think of the right adverb. What's going on inside their heads is much richer and more fulfilling than anything that might be happening in the outside world, whatever that may be.

Log-rolling

Anyone who has ever reviewed a book will know this term, which refers to the habit of puffing up your friends' books in reviews without ever actually mentioning that they're your friends, that you had dinner together last week and that you're godfather to their second son. It happens a lot, and each year *Private Eye* collects some of the worst examples and lists them on their Log-Rollers of the Year page.

And yet ... and yet ...

I had a book out a few years ago that died a death commercially, for no one was interested in it at all. (It's my worst-seller by a margin.) A few people I know, though, said how wonderful it was and deserved to do much better. So why don't you review it? said I. Oh I can't, they responded as one, you're a friend of mine. That would be log-rolling. What if it were? I asked between clenched teeth. No, it's more than my job's worth, they all said. If I were caught there would be hell to pay.

And so the book stiffed, unmourned by anyone except me.

I'm still angry about it, although to be fair, they may just have been lying. They may have thought the book was lousy but were telling me how brilliant it was just to avoid hurting my feelings. In which case not reviewing it, as they would have had to own up how bad the book really was, was an act of kindness.

But I don't buy that. For one thing, the book was not lousy at all, but a work of unalloyed genius, whose small but manifest flaws I intend to iron out in a second edition. Whenever I mention this to my publisher, his eyes glaze over and he quickly changes the subject.

No, I think they told the truth. They genuinely fear being done for log-rolling, and they believe that because I am connected to *Private Eye*, I would be fair game for Log-Rollers of the Year as they always include their own. Which they do, partly out of fairness but mostly out of mischief. There is much to be said for mischief.

The column appears every December, and while reading last year's, I had an odd thought. Why wasn't I in it? I had done loads of log-rolling, and I hadn't been caught. Then I saw that the person who I suspect writes the column had mentioned *himself.* It's not a matter of shame to be mentioned in this column. It's a matter of pride, masquerading as shame.

If we think about this from a slightly different angle, how do writers make friends among other writers? They go to book launches, they meet people and, very occasionally, they meet someone whose work they really like. Even more occasionally, that person likes your work in return. You have thus formed a mutual appreciation society. How on earth are you not going to become friends? Most of us are writing in a vacuum, seemingly unappreciated by all but our parents and a few maniacs on Amazon. To meet someone who genuinely enjoys what you do, and understands what you are going through day by day because he or she does it too, is beyond rubies.

The longer you work as a writer, the more likely it is that you are going to become friends with other writers, some of whom will have read and liked your work. So when you produce something new, who else are you going to show it to than one of your writer friends, who might then say he or she can't review it because you are friends? This is why I review my friends' work at every opportunity, because I am qualified to do so because I know and like their previous work. I usually mention that I know them in the copy, and this is usually cut out by the subs to avoid accusations of log-rolling. Can't be too careful.

Enemies

Well, we all have those. Even people much nicer than me.

When you're young, you write with a certain wild freedom and absolutely no thought for the future. Who cares if you rub a few people up the wrong way? Well, *you* might, if at some point in the future those people find themselves in positions of power and responsibility where they can do you down. Everyone forgets a good review of their work, but no one forgets a stinker. I remember three at least partially disobliging reviews of my books, all of them at least fifteen years old, and to quote an old Klingon proverb, revenge is a dish best served cold. In a long career, almost all of it forgotten by you the writer, you are *certain* to have upset a number of people who will henceforth and forever after want you dead. Some you will know about, but more dangerous are the enemies you don't know about. I have a friend who is a novelist of some standing, who has spent much of the past twenty years being carelessly disobliging about fellow writers in print. This fellow's novels are really good and always favourably reviewed, but they are never shortlisted for major awards. My friend is furious, as well he might be. But you only need one enemy on each selection panel to kill your book completely, and this fellow has pissed off so many people over so many years that one enemy per panel might be understating it some.

I'm not sure I have many enemies like that, probably because

I am not important enough to have them: only if you have more sway than I have ever had do you start to acquire them.* But I do have one or two good ones, and I shall tell you about one here. Picture the scene. It is slightly more than twenty years ago and I am writing regular book reviews for *Wisden Cricket Monthly*. The book that comes under my gaze is some piece of nonsense by the cricket commentator Henry Blofeld, possibly called *Cakes and Bails*, although it may have been even less funny than that. I have never met Blofeld, but I have always disliked his commentary, and it is with some glee that I realise that his book is truly dire: self-indulgent, viciously complacent, abysmally written, and going on and on about how wonderful his life is. I let fly. The review is printed without a single word being changed.

As the magazine is published, England are competing for the Ashes in Australia, and in the press box in Melbourne, copies of the magazine are passed around and sniggered at. Blofeld may be hugely popular with the cricketing public but his antics go down less well with fellow journalists. At which point Blofeld himself comes in and asks what's going on. Someone shows him the offending article.

The following day he has a heart attack.

Whenever I'm going to a lunch where I think he might be present, I ask to sit as far away from him as possible.

Excuses for missing deadlines

(All these gleaned from a master of the art.)

- Computer failure. Modern equivalent to 'the dog ate my homework'. Particularly depressing if this actually happens to you, because no one will ever believe you.

---

* Things might be different after this book comes out. That would be fun, wouldn't it?

- Feigning illness. One writer I know has pulled this one so often he now worries he is technically dead.
- 'It'll be with you by teatime.' Not only winningly cosy but, crucially, vague enough to mean anything between four and half past five. (Six o'clock at a pinch.)
- 'I emailed that to you an hour ago.' Sometimes true, sometimes not. If not true, you have about twenty minutes' grace in which to finish your piece and file it. Or possibly, start your piece and file it.
- 'You have reached the voicemail of Marcus Berkmann. Please speak after the tone.' If done live, must be done to perfection, without a scintilla of desperation or fear.

Working for free

You must never, EVER write anything for free, other than invoices, Christmas cards and shopping lists. Just the thought that I might be writing for free slows me down to a crawl. My last note to the milkman took me about twenty minutes.

The single exception is the occasional favour for a friend. Someone's doing a cheapy website, or a literary magazine, and they have no money, and they want five hundred words on something you know a lot about: that's OK. Everything else must be charged for. You're not writing for 'exposure'; you're writing for hard cash. Almost always, the person asking you to work for free is being paid to ask you, which makes you a mug if you say yes. Radio is notorious for this, because it appeals to the writer's vanity, despite the fact that no one will hear you speak or ever know that you have spoken, and you will have done all that work for nothing. But if you say no, they know that someone else, the next idiot on their list, will say yes. No money will have been spent, and the producers and presenters will have a nice jolly pub lunch on the proceeds. If you are wavering, this is a good thought to have in your head.

Increasingly controversial, it seems, are literary festivals. There are many of these, some rich, some poor, and it's best to know which is which. If you are going to the Hay Festival, which in the past has paid tens of thousands of pounds to Bill Clinton for doing a forty-minute speech, then you will want to be paid as well (£100 or £150 is acceptable). The smaller and more modest festivals I am happy to do for free, although a decent hotel room and getting my train fare reimbursed are essential. The funny thing is that I usually sell a lot of books at the smaller festivals and none at all at the larger festivals, which can be miserable experiences if you are only someone who writes books and not Ant or Dec. But if the smaller festival does offer to pay you, the answer is always 'Yes.' Or maybe 'Yes! Yes! Yes! Yes!' Give them your bank details before they change their minds.

Tax

My friend Louis put this on Facebook last January: 'If you're wondering about the economics of being a fairly obscure non-fiction author in 2020, I'm currently a little too cock-a-hoop about the forthcoming two-month holiday in council tax payments.' This, I feel, perfectly sums up most writers' feelings about their invariably parlous financial situation, and if anything, understates it for comic effect. Most of us feel about money the way a passenger in an aircraft feels when it goes into a steep dive it's unlikely to get out of: screaming terror and absolute powerlessness. I always thought I was quite an intelligent person until one day I decided that I was going to fill in my own tax return. This was after I had sorted out the probate for a dead relative, which involves filling in an absurd number of forms. How difficult could a tax return be? I soon found out. It's like trying to fly the space shuttle when you have successfully ridden a bicycle.

Certain dates are imprinted on the minds of every writer. April

5th is the end of the tax year. January 31st is when you have to pay the first half of your income tax to HMRC. July 31st is when you have to pay the second half. Some writers have the money saved up to pay this tax, sometimes months before it has to be coughed up. J. K. Rowling is one. Everybody else is frantically invoicing magazines and newspapers in the weeks before the deadline, borrowing money, remortgaging their house for the umpteenth time and selling their children to the white slave trade, a desperate move because, tragically, you can do it only once. I am writing this on January 11th, so I have twenty days to find the last couple of thousand I need. My overdraft is four hundred pounds short of its limit, but I have just bunged in a mighty invoice for some work I did in December, so I should be all right. I have been here many times before, but it gets no better, and I have run perilously close to the wire before. There were a few years when a particularly brutal gas bill could bring the whole edifice crumbling down. Somehow I have always got through, but the anxiety can be overpowering.

That I know exactly how much tax to pay is because I employ an accountant to tell me. This sounds very grand, but the tax return is so complicated and terrifying there really is no alternative. My accountant has traditionally charged me about £600 plus VAT for doing (in probably about an afternoon) what I could not do (in a month of Sundays), and every year I resent paying this enormous sum, which could be frittered away on luxuries like food and clothes. But my accountant trained long and hard to do easily what I can't do at all, rather as I charge as much as I can get away with for every writing job I get, on the basis that others would do it worse. Our skillsets are complementary but equivalent. Expertise is always worth paying for, and by writing the cheque you are effectively thanking him for all the intense boredom he has experienced in becoming an accountant so that you didn't have to. I tried mere gratitude, but he insisted on my sending the money as well.

The January 31st deadline concentrates the minds of many

writers, some of whom start sorting out their accounts as early as January 28th. We talk enough about procrastinating when it comes to writing, but this is as nothing compared to the pitiful and abject vacillation when we have to do our accounts. Most writers collect their receipts (because relevant expenditure can be offset against tax, and therefore bring down the amount of tax you have to pay) in what has become the traditional manner, by putting them all in a plastic bag and kicking it under the desk. Some just hand this bag over to their accountants with tears of shame in their eyes. The accountants tut and charge them double. I am slightly more orderly than this, but not much. What has changed things enormously, though, is that my accountants have recently introduced a sliding scale of charges to discourage their clients from their usual fluffy incompetence. If you hand in your accounts in January, as I always used to, you now pay £1300 plus VAT. If you get them in before the end of the previous September, though, this falls to £500 plus VAT. This has galvanised me to action, as nothing else could. Their purpose is simple: to make their own Januarys slightly less stressful and spread the work more evenly across the year. I assumed that everyone would be like me and ridiculously anxious to save as much money as possible, but my accountant told me that many of his self-employed clients still submit their accounts at the last possible moment. So to add to the misery caused by preventable procrastination, an enormous bill. That would probably give me a stroke.

What's particularly unfair about all this is that the number-crunchers at HMRC don't really understand how freelance life works, because if they did, they wouldn't have the rules they have. As wage slaves themselves, they operate on the assumption that everyone is a bit like them, the last refuge of the unimaginative since time immemorial. But our incomes wax and wane, sometimes ridiculously, almost unbelievably so. If I earn more than £50,000 one year, I expect to pay a fair amount of tax and do so, not with pleasure exactly, but with the grim resignation of the powerless. But on January 31st, freelances aren't paying the tax for the year that ended the previous April, they're paying, on account, for the year that ends the following April. HMRC assumes you'll make the same amount as you made the previous year, and charges you accordingly. But what if, in the meantime, your income has dropped to £20,000? The only recourse is to ask your accountant to beg for a reduction in the tax you will have to pay, which may not work as HMRC may think you are lying. Even if you are lying, you will only have to pay an even larger amount the following year. The figures, I have to admit, make my eyes water. The only real consolation is that my rich non-writer friends are actually paying less tax than I am, because they have all their money stashed in the Cayman Islands, where they have a small army of sabre-toothed accountants working on their behalf. When they offer to pay for lunch I always remember this, and then say yes with a beaming smile.

Getting paid

It is getting increasingly hard to get paid for anything.

Not long ago I had written a piece for new client, a magazine of long standing and sound reputation. I wrote it and sent it off, they liked it, and within a week I had been invited to send in an invoice. Swift work, I thought. It was for a reasonable amount, too.

No payment arrived. Ten days later I received an email from the assistant saying I needed a purchase order number. Could I wait a day or two for the purchase order number and then resubmit the invoice, only this time with my inside leg measurement and favourite colour added to the bank details, email address, phone numbers and all the rest? OK, I said, no worries.

The purchase order number arrived within forty-eight hours, and I resubmitted.

Still no payment.

Two weeks later I got a phone call from an eastern European woman in a call centre. She was from Blah Blah Media Ltd and could she have my bank details? No, I said, and slammed the phone down. Bloody scammers.

Half an hour later I received an email from Olga at Blah Blah Media Ltd asking for my bank details.

I emailed the assistant. Was this for real?

Sadly so, said the assistant. Although I had already put my bank details on the invoice, the company's auditors insisted that the company ring their contributors up to verify them. I rang Olga back. She laughed charmingly, possibly because I was not the first, or even the twenty-first, person who had slammed the phone down on her today.

As I write, it's two weeks since that phone call, and I am still waiting for payment. My guess is that it has gone direct to a drug cartel's bank account in Bolivia, and that Russian heavies are currently emptying my own bank account of every penny that isn't actually in there, as my overdraft is still close to its limit.

In the meantime I spoke to an auditor of my acquaintance, and asked him about that.

His considered professional response was 'That's bollocks'.

A while ago I was rung up by a languid posh bloke from *The Times*. He was one of those men whose vowels sound as though they have been hung on washing lines overnight. He asked me if I fancied writing a humorous piece for Saturday's paper. Nine hundred words, five hundred quid. Yes, I said, trying not to scream. That would do.

I wrote the piece, which went in and looked wonderful. They had found a picture of me from somewhere in which I actually looked alive. They hadn't changed a word. I rejoiced.

The following Tuesday I sent an email to the languid posh bloke thanking him, and telling him that loads of my friends had seen the piece, which they had. He sent me back a shirty one-liner: 'Yes, people usually say that when they've been published by *The Times*.' If we were being kind, he was just having a bad day.

I gave him a week to kick his pets around the house and then rang him back. But I was too late. In the intervening week he had been sacked. 'Languid Posh Bloke no longer works here' was the official line, but I know the way newspapers work.

What had happened? Had this man's career had been progressing smoothly until he commissioned me to write a piece? I imagined him being summoned to the editor's office on Monday and asked to explain why he had printed such a thorough-going piece of shit from me. After all, humour is in the eye of the beholder. *The Times* isn't exactly renowned for its knockabout gags and jolly chortles. Was I responsible for the end of this man's career?

I sent emails, trying to get paid. Emails gave me phone numbers, which I rang and which never seemed to be answered. I could speak to no one who had responsibility, or who cared, or who could do anything. I just wanted my £500, but the demise of Languid Posh Bloke had apparently sealed off even the possibility of payment. Although my piece had been in the paper accompanied by a photo clearly of me, he hadn't done the paperwork and no one else could be arsed to do it in his stead.

Four years later, I have almost given up on being paid for this piece, but not entirely. In a way, one of the reasons I would like this book to succeed is so that *The Times* might ring me up and offer me some work, and I would say, pay me the £500 you owe me, or fuck off.

13

Construction

'Writers usually find some excuse for their books, although why one should excuse oneself for having such a quiet and peaceful occupation I really don't know.'

Leonora Carrington, The Hearing Trumpet

How do we construct one of these pieces? Where do the 610 words of deathless prose come from?

There are two answers to this, neither of them very helpful. Nobody knows. And everybody's different.

I just sit there, stare out of the window for a while, and wait for the first sentence to arrive. As I said before, it doesn't matter whether or not that first sentence is any good, because the chances are it will never appear in the finished piece. One of the oldest tricks in journalism is that the first paragraph can almost always go. It's either irrelevant or too gentle an entry into what you were thinking of writing. Far better is to leap in straight away. How did I start this chapter? With the sentence 'How do we construct one of these pieces?' It's what the chapter is about. Why hang about?

Everybody is different because our working methods have all adapted to suit our personalities. I think these things are set quite early. For instance, when you were at school writing an essay, did you construct a detailed essay plan before you started writing? Some people do; some people have to. But I never did, because even then the reason for writing the essay was to find out what I knew and thought about the subject. I didn't know everything I knew, and I often didn't know what I thought, although I often thought I knew what I thought I knew. It was much easier to lie to the teacher and pretend I had done an essay plan, which took only marginally more time than just not doing an essay plan. This is probably why, at university, I ended up doing maths.

You may not realise this, because I look so young, but Nigella Lawson was at the same university as me at the same time as me. For a while, many years ago before she achieved wider fame, she had a weekly column in the *Observer* about politics, which drove me mad because it read like a sixth-form essay: clunky, dull and over-planned. Why didn't I have a column like that? Because, bluntly, I wasn't Nigella Lawson and she was. But she is no fool, and in time she reinvented herself as a wonderful writer on food and became globally renowned. And I ceased to resent her because she had made what she could of what she had, which is all any of us can do.

So no essay plan then, and no essay plan now. Just start and see where it takes you. As I write this, I have not the slightest idea where this chapter is going. I'll find out soon, I hope.

The only real rule about writing columns is that, ideally, the last sentence or two should make some slightly strange and unexpected reference to what you said earlier in the piece: the twist in the tail. Almost everyone does this to some extent, but I'm not sure anyone does it more skilfully than Nicholas Lezard in his Down and Out column in the *New Statesman*. I have talked about this with him and he does the same thing as I do. He writes the thing, he gets to the end and, because the deadline is looming and the bailiffs are at the door, he thinks of the twist at the last possible moment. One of the greatest pleasures of writing one of these twists is making it look as though the piece was always going to end there, that there was a sort of inevitability about it, whereas in truth you never had a clue what you were going to do and the sentence just came to you when it had to. This is certainly exciting, but the stress of it can get to you after thirty years or so, which may explain why so many writers are smoking cigarettes out of every orifice, except for their mouths, into which they are currently pouring a generous whisky and soda.

So what are you trying to say? If you too are a humorous writer, the temptation is to shove in as many jokes as you can, just because you can. I was guilty of this when I was younger, but less so now. This was the greatest lesson I learned while writing my disastrous script with Richard, the film-director-turned-life-coach. Everything in the script, said Richard, has to do some work. If it's not actually helping the plot or the characters progress, it has to go. This is probably why I hate Quentin Tarantino's films so much, because almost alone of current filmmakers, he has long digressive scenes of dialogue that simply do not need to be there. They stay because Quentin likes them. Really, the man is lucky to be alive, but instead they give him ever more awards and money with which to make even more terrible films. All of which is strictly irrelevant to what we were talking about, and should really be excised. Remind me: I'll do it later.

Every joke needs to do some work. Again, read Lezard's columns if you want to know how to do this, but the true master is the American humorist David Sedaris, who actually makes very few jokes, and every single one of them counts. One reason for this is that every essay of his, before it goes into print, is rigorously tested in front of an audience. If a joke doesn't work, it goes – and that's 'work' in both senses: help the narrative in some way, and make people laugh.

The other priority, whether you are writing humorously or not, is some level of originality. I figure that in any 610-word piece I need to make at least two or three genuinely original observations. More, if you can. If you are just writing what everyone else is writing, you are literally wasting your time. You also need to vary your subject matter, even a little. A few geniuses, like the late Auberon Waugh, can write almost exactly the same piece every week for a quarter of a century, and still make them all fresh and funny and interesting, but only a few. There's a writer I read who writes every single column on race and racism. She writes well, and obviously racism is horrible, but the sheer monotony of her pieces makes me want to scream. For a while I just thought she must be obsessed, which would be understandable, but more recently I have begun to wonder whether she isn't just pigeonholed by her newspaper as a writer on racism. And if so, isn't it actually racist to pigeonhole a black writer as a writer on racism? If I met her I might ask her, although I suspect she might think it was racist to wonder whether it was racist to pigeonhole her as a writer on racism.

Why humour? That's a very good question. There's a screenwriting guru whose name I have forgotten, the sort who charges people hundreds of dollars to attend his seminars, who says that all humour is based on rage. Which seems to me the sort of bilge you say when you are an eminent screenwriting guru who hasn't had any screenplays produced. All humour is based on rage, except for all the humour that isn't. As it happens, I write humorously because – and this may sound bizarre – it's much easier than writing seriously. It feels like dancing rather than walking. We can't all be Fred Astaire, but it's something to aspire to. Writing without jokes, by contrast, is hard bloody work. (This is probably what I mean about everyone being different.) For me, humour oils the wheels of life. I wrote earlier about becoming friends with Ian Hislop, and how do you think that happened? We met in a mutual friend's rooms in college; we made each other laugh; the friendship formed in that instant.

Of course there are people who say that humour isn't serious, and seriousness (which is to say humourlessness) is more important somehow, more *serious*. Such people tend to become judges of literary prizes or editors of national newspapers that once employed me.

All writers, comic or not, share one attribute: discipline. As my friend Amanda says, you just have to sit down and get on with it. Bum on seat. Pen on paper, or fingers on keyboard. Neil Gaiman has his Eight Rules for Writing, which include the following:

> *3. Finish what you're writing. Whatever you have to do to finish it, finish it.*
> *4. Put it aside. Read it pretending you've never read it before. Show it to friends whose opinion you respect and who like the kind of thing that this is.*
> *5. Remember: when people tell you something's wrong or doesn't work for them, they are almost always right. When they tell you exactly what they think is wrong and how to fix it, they are almost always wrong.*
> *6. Fix it. Remember that, sooner or later, before it ever reaches perfection, you will have to let it go and move on and start to write the next thing. Perfection is like chasing the horizon. Keep moving.*

They are all good, but 5 is genius.

We have discussed the beginnings and the ends of articles, and slightly skated over the middles, because, bizarrely, they're usually the easiest bit to write. Let's assume that you know roughly what you want to say, either consciously (you have a plan) or subconsciously (you haven't). So start writing. Only when you have written something can you see what works and what doesn't, what is to the point and what is irrelevant, and which bits should go in which order. This latter may seem ridiculously trivial but it's actually one of the hardest things to get right. Time after time, I have been staring at a piece I have written and am thinking, this isn't quite right, and then I realise, hang on, this bit needs to go there, which means this bit isn't necessary any more, and so on. At the eleventh hour, the piece rewrites itself and your job is done.

Also, you do not need to say anything twice. Saying something twice is one more time than you need to say anything.

This isn't strictly a writing guide, so I'm not going to give any rules of what to write and what not to write. Well, not many, anyway. Primarily, though, your job as a writer is not to annoy the reader. Thus, avoid words that don't mean anything. If you use the word 'iconic' to mean 'actually quite decent', at least a third of your readers will instantly stop reading. Overuse has dulled the word irrevocably. Try not to start too many sentences with 'so'. (I have a habit of starting my sentences with 'And so'. I have to go through everything I write and cut them out.) Avoid genteelisms: long words that sound 'better' than short words, but really aren't. Any writer who habitually uses 'commence' instead of 'start' or 'begin' should be regarded with suspicion. The absolute worst, a neologism of the past few years which all people in management seem to use, in speech and in writing, is to tack on the words 'going forward' at the end of a sentence. 'I really think we need to consider this, going forward.' When an old friend I had previously trusted started saying things like this to me in all seriousness, I knew I had lost him. It's utter bullshit, and really there is an argument that anyone using it without irony should be picked off by snipers hiding on the roofs of surrounding buildings for the very purpose.

Writing experts generally say that you should avoid clichés like the plague, but I don't think that's necessarily true. For instance, I used the phrase 'at the eleventh hour' a couple of paragraphs ago, and I'll bet you didn't even notice. If I had used a more unusual phrase, it might have detracted from what I was trying to say. Clichés can also be fun to play with or subvert. I have an old friend who never stops talking, and whose every anecdote can last fifteen or twenty minutes unless you choose that moment to go to the loo. Donkeys in his town, I told a mutual friend, must learn to operate without hind legs.

Finally, the big one: the split infinitive. Every time I split an infinitive in print, I get at least one letter from a madman who says I should be instantly deported back to where I came from (Hampstead). People who know nothing about anything, let alone how to write a coherent sentence, know that you should never split an infinitive. I would cite, in evidence against, the sentence of fond memory 'To boldly go where no man has gone before'. It's a good sentence, and both William Shatner and Patrick Stewart, in their voiceovers on *Star Trek*'s opening credits, make the most of it. Should it be 'Boldly to go', or 'To go boldly'? No, no, no, a thousand times no.

In fact, many writers much better than Gene Roddenberry split infinitives all over the place. Muriel Spark was a serial splitter. When I reply, witheringly, to the madmen, I quote as evidence the following (slightly edited) passage from Harry Fieldhouse's *Everyman's Good English Guide* (1982), which has more good sense within its hard covers than the Old Testament:

> *Split infinitives.* This is an old dispute which should have been settled long ago. The issue is whether a full infinitive such as *to be* should be interrupted (split) by an adverb as in *to suddenly be.* The practice is avoided by many writers under the impression that it is a grammatical offence or at least a stylistic lapse. It is certainly not a grammatical offence.
>
> Perhaps because a confident grasp of grammar is

uncommon among native speakers of English – a language that makes few demands for declensions and conjugations etc. – concern for whatever offences the ordinary person thinks he can recognise is all the more passionate. Split infinitives are one of these. A split infinitive can inflame the businessman who muddles his tenses and upset a politician who is blind to a *non sequitur*. This concern is the more extraordinary in that objectors can rarely explain why they object. Vague authority may be invoked, but the fact is that twentieth-century grammarians from Otto Jespersen onwards have dismissed the aversion as unfounded ...

The resistance may survive from the days when Latin was taken as the model for English. Dryden, the scourge of prepositions at the end of sentences, admittedly tested his English by translation into Latin, and Latin of course has neither prepositions at the end of sentences nor splittable infinitives. Explaining English in terms of Latin has been a traditional theme of grammarians. Old English had infinitives with a dative form, as in Latin, and *to* (which is a dative preposition) commemorates this in modern infinitives.

That however is an absurd reason for never separating it, since most English verb forms consist of two or more words, and we split them freely, as in 'scholars *will* always *quibble*'. Besides, there is more than one kind of infinitive. *To have asked* is as much an infinitive as to ask, yet we split the three words of *to have asked* – 'He was wise *to have* politely *asked*' – as a matter of routine. So why not the two words of *to ask* or *to have*?

Fowler, in giving guarded approval to splitting, fogged the point with an appeal to 'instinctive good taste'. Good taste, as Mae West said of goodness in relation to how she came by her big diamond, has nothing to do with it. But clarity has, and so has natural English rhythm. *To really learn a language you have to keep practising* is a clear and natural wording. If reworded as *Really to learn a language . . .* it would be affected. If reworded as *To learn a language really you have . . .* there would be doubt about which half of the sentence *really* was intended to intensify.

Should we all stop and think every time we want to say something like *I am anxious not to unduly burden you/ He is right to strongly oppose these changes*? Must we then take care to revise the sequence to . . . *anxious not to burden you unduly/ . . . right to oppose these changes strongly*? To seriously expect any such thing would be far-fetched even if grammar required it – and it does not.

I have probably sent this passage to twenty-five people over the years, and none of them has ever replied.

14

Flowery Twats

'Some writers take to drink, other writers take to audiences.'

Gore Vidal

Quizzes crept up on me when I wasn't looking. The first pub quiz I went to was at the Cock Tavern in Great Portland Street, London W1, back in 1991 or 1992, invited along by a group of comedy writers I knew. There's no one in the world more miserable than comedy writers, just as there's no one more drunk than cartoonists. But as we won most weeks, my team were only savagely gloomy rather than wrist-cuttingly morose, while I had chanced on a leisure activity that was going to change my life. I had always loved pubs, but here was an opportunity to love them even more, with some added showing-off when you were the only person on your team who knew the answer to question four. The Cock's Monday night quiz soon ended when the pub's landlord fled to Scotland in a hurry, but like Dracula after his first ingestion of human blood, I had developed a taste for it. I searched long and hard for a suitable replacement in north London where I live, and after a long and arduous journey, I found the Tuesday night quiz at the Prince of Wales in Highgate. Twenty-five years later, I'm still going.

As I get older, I find my cultural range has narrowed. I long since gave up pretending that I wanted to go to another opera, and these days I barely ever go to the theatre. Having been a television obsessive, I hardly watch anything any more, but if you tell me there's some shitty quiz in a nearby pub tomorrow night, I'll probably be there, bright-eyed, holding my pen and ready for action. Most pub quizzes are, of course, terrible, as they are extracted from the internet at minimal cost and feature the same boring old questions as all other quizzes. Who did win the League Cup in 1972? I neither know nor care. But a few rare quizzes break through the quality barrier and these are the ones you must cherish. In the Prince of Wales, by ancient tradition, the various regular teams take it in turns to set the quiz, and as well as competing furiously to win when they are taking part, they compete furiously to present the best possible quiz when they are at the business end of the microphone. A few teams go too far and make their quizzes too hard, and accordingly the PoW has developed a reputation as the hardest quiz in London, which isn't quite deserved. The quizzes some of us set are kinder than that. The quality varies hugely but every quizmaster works diligently at his or her questions, so even when it doesn't quite work, every quiz has an individual flavour to it. There may well be harder quizzes in London, but if there's a better one I would be surprised.

This is a book about writing, and it will amaze you not to learn that I quickly became obsessed with the craft of writing quiz questions. It's not dissimilar to writing haikus, or even jokes: they have to be small and perfectly formed, and timing is everything. If you know the answer, all well and good. If you can work out the answer from the clues in the question, even better. And if you get the answer wrong but you desperately want to know what the right answer is, that's also good. The main thing is that the question should never be designed to make the quizmaster look clever. That's to miss the point completely. Quizzes, like book reviews, are an entertainment. If they do not please and/or amuse the punters, they are nothing.

What was otherwise known as Watery Fowls, Flay Otters, Fatty Owls, Flowery Twats and Farty Towels?

Dead easy if you know it, but also quite easy to work out, as they are all partial anagrams of the show's title, *Fawlty Towers*. (These were the signs outside the hotel in the last five episodes.) I like this question because it's funny and unexpected, but mainly because it's straightforward and pretty much two guaranteed points for everyone.

Penguin, flummery, flannel, coracle and corgi are five of the relatively few words in English known to be taken from which language?

The answer is Welsh and the big clue there is corgi, of which there are two types, the Pembroke Welsh corgi and the Cardigan Welsh corgi. So the answer is unlikely to be Latin or Basque. Other words which may or may not be taken from Welsh (i.e. some etymologists dispute this) are flimsy, maggot and balderdash.

In the painting, what is the Mona Lisa's right hand resting on?

This one was written by my old friend and quizzing brother Chris Pollikett, who died in 2016. I love it because, as soon as you're asked it, your mind goes completely blank and you realise you haven't a clue. Until you realise, maybe only half a second later, that the only possible thing her right hand could be resting on is her left hand.

The Test cricketer, Southampton and England footballer, diplomat, sailor and literary critic C. B. Fry: which athletic world record did he equal in 1892?

Easy if you know it – the answer is the long jump – but amusing if you don't. Quizzers will forgive a lot if you make them smile.

I have a lingering fondness for binary questions, i.e. questions that have two and only two possible answers. You can only put a handful of such questions in each quiz because they are apt to drive people mad.

Which is wider, Australia or the Moon?

Could you get any simpler than that? The answer is Australia, but only by a handful of miles, and it's important to mention this as you give the answer, as it tells everyone something they didn't previously know and will never forget for the rest of their lives: that the Moon is roughly the same size as Australia.

The big question, the one we are always asking ourselves is: is there such a thing as the perfect quiz question? I really hope so, and after a quarter of a century writing quiz questions, I think I have come across it. It is this:

Who is older, Gary Oldman or Gary Numan?

You can tell that this is a cast-iron classic, because it's now asked rather often and everyone thinks they thought of it first. I think I thought of it first, and I am almost certainly right.

The answer is even better than the question, because Gary Numan is older than Gary Oldman, but only by thirteen days (8 March 1958 compared to 21 March 1958). This is a fact that should be part of the architecture of everyone's mind. A small buttress, perhaps, or maybe a gargoyle.

How to make money from all this? This is a question that often goes through a writer's mind, especially when he's enjoying himself. How can I make this pleasurable activity make me some cash? I have long made a habit of writing professionally about my interests, because there are bills to pay, cats to be fed, small children to turn into large greedy children and crumbling window sills to be, frankly, left alone to crumble some more because there's always something more important to spend the money on. There *had* to be some money in quizzes, surely?

Quiz books, as we saw earlier, do not sell. My quizzing friend

Chris had similar ambitions, so we sat in pubs trying to come up with brilliant schemes that would make us rich. We thought of supplying our questions to pubs via the internet, but of the (now) 23,000 pubs that do regular quizzes, around 22,750 were either writing the questions themselves (no use to anyone) or paying buttons for questions written by starving quiz slaves who had probably started out like us, with dreams of unimaginable wealth, power and kidney-shaped swimming pools.

With a third friend we started a company, named after my book *Brain Men*, to write and present quizzes for clients who were, preferably, loaded. We actually ran this company with moderate success for a few years, but I found I was writing and presenting between sixty and seventy quizzes a year for only slightly more money, all told, than I received for writing a monthly film column for the *Oldie*. And doing these quizzes, mainly for suited shits in the City of London, who get drunk and cheat wildly and ask you to repeat question five for the fourteenth time because they were too busy looking up the answer to the previous question on Google to bother to listen, became more than simply a chore, but something to be dreaded wholeheartedly. I sold my share of the company and went back to doing quizzes mainly for fun.*

The lesson we learned from Brain Men is that, sadly, not everything you like can be magically transformed into teetering piles of money. For a while there I had a 'portfolio career', a wonderfully grand term that suggests that you have more than one way of making a living and, indeed, are thinking of new ways all the time. Freelances are particularly good at this – at suggesting or implying that they are making a fortune, rather than actually making a fortune. I have a writer acquaintance who is always telling me how well he is doing, of his great plans, and how he's just 'this far' from making a mint and retiring to Barbados to be

---

* Note use of the word 'mainly'. If someone waves a suitably sized cheque in front of my nose, I rarely say no.

waited on by handmaidens. And yet I know for a fact that this man has eaten nothing but Spam since a week last Wednesday. The poor guy has even started *smelling* of Spam.

But things have a way of working out, and often in the most surprising ways. In 2005, with two friends, I entered a Radio 4 show called *Masterteam*. We didn't do very well, but I did meet the show's producer, Paul Bajoria, who runs almost all of Radio 4's quiz output. I liked him and he must have liked me, because a few years later he rang me up. Fred Housego needed knee surgery and so wouldn't be available to record the next series of *Round Britain Quiz*. Would I like to stand in for him?

I hummed and hahed. All I knew about *Round Britain Quiz* was that the questions were extraordinarily difficult, which probably meant they were far too difficult for me. I rang Chris, and he said, do it. You'll never regret it. What have you got to lose?

Well, my dignity, my reputation, I said.

You lost those years ago, said Chris.

I rang Paul back and said yes. It was one of the best decisions I ever made.

It's called 'Round Britain' because there are six teams of two people each, from Scotland, Wales, Northern Ireland, North of England, Midlands and South of England. The teams change surprisingly little from year to year, because that's the way the game has always been played, but also because most people get better at the quiz the longer they play it. In that first year I was teamed with Marcel Berlins, a rackety old journalist in his early seventies who, for a while, wrote the excellent weekly quiz in the *Guardian*'s *Weekend* magazine. Marcel suggested we meet for a drink to acquaint ourselves, so we sat outside the Charlotte Street Hotel in late summer and drank rather a lot of wine. I liked him. He had clearly been round the block once or twice and had some useful advice for the quiz we were about to face, which was: don't worry, you can't revise, you either know it or you don't, the worst that can happen is that you look a complete fool, but that's the show. And he said this that stayed with me: the contestants aren't as important as the questions. Our job is to answer these questions to the best of our ability and if we don't know the answers, well, tough.

All excellent advice, and I prepared for the forthcoming ordeal not by listening to the CDs of the last series that Paul had so kindly sent me, but by not listening to them. A clear mind is an open mind. Or rather, it's a mind that isn't going to vomit on the floor with terror as soon as the first question is asked.

The series is always recorded at a hotel in the middle of nowhere, without an audience, in a room specifically put aside for the purpose, and all twelve shows are done in under three days. This may sound extravagant but it's actually much cheaper than inviting everyone up to Salford (where the programme is based) to record it in a studio. (Such is the arcane and incomprehensible nature of the BBC's finances.) The fact that this also makes it a much more civilised and enjoyable experience for the contestants is pure coincidence. The 2012 series was recorded in a slightly shabby hotel in the County Antrim countryside, and when I reached it I met the other contestants, all but two of them older than me and most of them far more eminent in their fields. There were academics, biographers, proper broadsheet journalists, at least one winner of a million pounds on *Who Wants to Be a Millionaire?*, rackety Marcel and me. It was, as they say, a motley old crew, but they were all unusually friendly, to me and to each other, and almost all of them had scabrous tales to tell about the man I was temporarily replacing, Fred Housego, the London cabbie whose victory in the 1980 series of *Mastermind* had generated a stellar media career. None of these stories, sadly, can I retell here, as he is still alive and probably has recourse to lawyers. But my ears quickly went red and stayed that way for the duration of the recording.

The teams on *RBQ* can be on such good terms because we are not really competing against each other. We are competing against the questions. If you have a question that's so tough you lose the match because of it, everyone is sympathetic afterwards because at some point the same thing has happened to them. There's also an element of the lottery about the show, because not everyone plays everyone else. Each team plays two of the other teams twice, and the other three teams not at all. This is basically for scheduling reasons, because some team members are so busy they can only make certain days of the recording and they want to get their matches over as soon as possible. I am not at all busy, so I want to arrive as early as possible, leave as late as possible and go for as many long walks as I can manage in between.

So, to the questions. There are only eight questions in each half-hour programme, four per team. They are complicated and abstruse, and they use parts of the brain you didn't know you had. Here's one Marcel and I had in my first year, on my first show, no less:

Who might have travelled Hopefully to the Lion City, Unguja, Rabat, Amaurote, Cidade Maravilhosa, Denpasar and the Fragrant Harbour?

We each get our four questions on pieces of paper at the beginning of the recording, just after the theme tune has played. The first one you may only have seconds to solve (depending on which team's turn it is to go first). The fourth and last you have the whole half-hour to ponder, and you may need every second of that. It does help seeing them on paper, because I'm not a particularly verbal person and I find it easier to take in information I am reading rather than I am being told. (Listeners can now look up the questions on the show's website, which I would recommend.) This question depends on the capital letter in 'Hopefully', although it took us rather too long to work that out. Rabat, we both knew, is the capital of Morocco, and the Fragrant Harbour is a nickname for Hong Kong. When we realised that 'Hopefully' was a reference to Bob Hope, the question unravelled. These, then, were the locations of the 'Road to . . .' films, starring Bob Hope and Bing Crosby, and made between 1940 and 1962. Marcel remembered that *The Road to Hong Kong* was the last one of the series, so this meant they were in chronological order, *Road to Singapore* (the literal meaning of which is 'lion city'), *Road to Zanzibar* (Unguja is the largest island there), *Road to Morocco*, *Road to Utopia* (Amaurote, or Amaurot, is the capital city of Utopia in Thomas More's book), *Road to Rio* ('Cidade Maravilhosa' is a march written for the Rio de Janeiro festival of 1935 and now adopted as the city's anthem) and *Road to Bali* (Denpasar is the capital city).

See what I mean?

If you knew all that and could explain it clearly enough to sat-isfy the Olympian standards of the show's host, Tom Sutcliffe, you would get six points out of six. We didn't know the order of the films, and we obviously had no idea about the specific relevance of many of the foreign terms, so we hummed and hahed and guessed wildly and I think we got three points. After a question like that you would ideally have a shower and a nap. We had a cup of tea and then recorded the next show.

People say the questions are impossible, and of course they are, but it really helps that there are two of you, and it helps even more if your knowledge and your talents complement each other's. As the recording progressed, it became clear that Marcel and I didn't gel particularly well as a team. We had very similar general knowledge, geared shamelessly towards popular culture, so we tended to know the same things and be dumbfounded by the same things. Fred Housego and Marcel had been a much better mix. It also became clear to me that, as one of the most competitive men in Britain, Marcel saw me less as a teammate than as a personal threat. Teammates on the show work things out quietly, off air, and then agree to share the glory, if you like, when it's your turn on the mike. But Marcel, when he knew something, was straight in there like a ferret up a trouser leg, and when he didn't know the answer, he would go completely silent, as though he had taken Trappist vows or fallen into a short but hopefully deadly coma. I was left to fluff through as best I could, while he looked at me through the sides of his eyes with ill-concealed malevolence. It was a rather disturbing experience. Friends of mine who knew him better have spoken to me of his great personal kindness and generosity, and I don't disbelieve them, but I would say that none of them had been on a quiz show with him. By the fourth and last of the shows we recorded, I had learned not to give too much away of what I had worked out of a question, because I couldn't trust him not to take all the credit. This is not the way for a team to work.

Nonetheless, the last question we answered on the last show we recorded may have been our finest hour.

How would Sir Jimmy Savile have described a fondly remembered primate, a Walter Scott hero, the inventor of the Uzi and a unit of acceleration?

By extraordinary coincidence I had recently written a quiz question for the Prince of Wales about the Uzi gun, which I knew had been invented by an Israeli man called Uziel Gal. And the fondly remembered primate: was that Guy the Gorilla?

The fog began to clear. We seemed to be talking about Jimmy Savile's catchphrase, 'Guys and Gals'. It was time for some wild guesses. The unit of acceleration: could that be the gal, possibly named after Galileo? It could! Which meant that Walter Scott had called a novel *Guy Something*, although we didn't know what. (It's *Guy Mannering*: very hard, for us at least.) For this we got five out of six points. We were both immeasurably pleased by this.

But this was 2012. The autumn of 2012, to be precise.

Between the recording of the show, in October, and its broadcast date the following January, the grim truth about Jimmy Savile (who had died the previous year) became known. He had been a predatory sex offender over six decades, with both guys and gals, not all of them strictly alive. In panic mode, the BBC decided that a quiz question about him, however brilliantly answered by Marcel and me, was not acceptable fare for the Radio 4 audience. I disagreed strongly, but then we had got five points on the question. Paul Bajoria called Marcel and me into the BBC Theatre in London in early January to record a replacement question. I don't remember the replacement question and I don't want to remember it. Marcel and I got one point out of six and our small triumph of the previous autumn was officially airbrushed from *RBQ* history.

I have to admit that as I left the theatre, I felt more than a little deflated. Marcel, though, seemed cheerful enough. 'See you next year!' he said to the production team. He then turned to me and gave me a triumphant look, which meant 'Except for you.'

Fred Housego returned, but he and Marcel were beginning to struggle. I couldn't bear to listen, but Chris tuned in on my behalf and reported, with some glee, that their quizzing faculties were waning. Indeed, most of the older teams seemed to be in long-term decline. After the 2013 series the Scottish team, who had been there since before the Union with England, were sensationally retired (sacked) and replaced by the thriller writer Val McDermid and the poet Roddy Lumsden, both young sprites in their fifties. When these two won their first series the following year, it was the excuse Paul needed to start a spring clean of the teams, before they all died of old age. Marcel and Fred, both now in their seventies, were the next to go, and Paul rang up to ask if I fancied taking part again. This time I was rather quicker to say yes.

My partner for the 2015 series was Simon Singh, the science writer and particle physicist who, among other things, had been sued for libel by the British Chiropractic Association and rather wonderfully won his case. I had loved his book about Fermat's Last Theorem, and was keen to meet him, although he turned out to be rather nervous about doing the show, which surprised me, given his giant brain and the amount of broadcasting he had done. As it happens, we were lucky in our opposition and won the series by the narrowest of margins, but Simon decided against returning the following year, saying he would spend the summer dreading the recording and it wasn't worth the angst. I myself, rather more frivolous than he is, would spend the rest of the year desperately looking forward to the recording, but each to his own.

His replacement was Paul Sinha, stand-up comedian, qualified doctor and one of the Chasers on the ITV quiz show *The Chase*, and one of the few contestants to bring his partner, now husband, Oliver, to the recording every year. Paul and I dovetail quite nicely. He knows everything about everything, especially sport and the Olympics. My general knowledge isn't a fraction as good as his, but I'm better at the lateral thinking part of the equation, so I often see the links in the questions more quickly. And sometimes it works the other way: I get the facts, he gets the links. It's a good partnership.

So here's a question Paul and I had in the series we recorded in late 2019:

If you're a regulator with no real powers, a bureaucrat who's anonymous and unaccountable, or someone who's drunk, in what sense might you sympathise with Samson in Gaza?

We looked at that for a while, I can tell you.

The way into it was to remember, as I did, that Aldous Huxley wrote a novel called *Eyeless in Gaza*. And Paul remembered that that was a quote from John Milton, which I would never have got. See the link now?

'Someone who's drunk' is legless.

'A bureaucrat who's anonymous and unaccountable' is faceless.

And we took a few moments to work out the last one, or rather the first one. Lots of racking of brains, and making humming noises to pass the time, and then Paul got it. 'A regulator with no real powers' is toothless. All parts of the body, or rather their lack. Six points.

The point-scoring system is a mystery to some listeners, because there's so much judgement involved. Six, as previously explained, is the maximum for each question, but you lose points whenever Tom Sutcliffe has to give you a nudge, or even a full solid barge. He is adept at steering you in the direction of the right answer, but it'll cost you. He and Paul Bajoria agree how many points to award for each question, and sometimes they don't agree at all, which is fun, although tragically this bit doesn't reach the listener. Marcel was famous for arguing robustly with the chair when he had felt he had been undermarked, but my own feeling is that marginal undermarking and overmarking all even out in the end, as long as you don't shout too loud.

Remember the Freelance Triangle? These are the three questions you should ask yourself whenever anyone contacts you and offers you some work. Is there any money in it? Is there job satisfaction? Is there kudos? If your answer to two of the three questions is yes, then you should go ahead. If your answer to only one of the three is yes, then you should politely decline. There are no jobs that give all three. Except that there is one: *Round Britain Quiz*.

Astoundingly, we are paid for this; not a huge sum, but enough. Job satisfaction is guaranteed, partly because the quiz itself is so enjoyable, and partly because you go to a country house hotel for a couple of days and it doesn't cost you anything. And kudos? If there's a cooler show to appear on on Radio 4, I don't know of it.

Here's one of my favourite questions, from a couple of years ago:

Why might a former Olympic field athlete throw a party, inviting the following guests? A furious Scotsman. An optimistic South African. A Chilean musician. A supporter of the Green Party resident in West Africa. And a Greenlander who was unable to stay very long.

It was the last question we had to answer, so we had nearly half an hour in which to solve it, but it hardly mattered, as we didn't have a clue. Paul pointed out that neither of us could name a single Chilean musician, so it was clearly some form of wordplay. But what?

We just sat and stared at it and waited for inspiration to strike. Then, roughly fifteen seconds before we were due on air, I got it.

'An optimistic South African' was the Cape of Good Hope.

'A Chilean musician' was therefore Cape Horn.

And 'a supporter of the Green Party resident in West Africa' was the westernmost point of Africa, Cape Verde. (Verde = green in Spanish.)

Paul immediately got the two hard ones. 'A furious Scotsman' is Cape Wrath, the most north-westerly point in mainland Britain. And 'a Greenlander who was unable to stay very long' was that country's southernmost tip, Cape Farewell.

And the former Olympic field athlete? Geoff Capes.

Bear in mind that we worked this out in almost absolute silence, because the other team were answering their own question at the time. Six points. I punched the air, very, very quietly.

15

A Short Drive Down the A12

'I don't do witty off-the-cuff remarks. It's like throwing £5 notes into the gutter.'

Keith Waterhouse

In the summer of 2015 my friend Simon O'Hagan rang up with some good news. He had been made editor of the *Independent Magazine*, a modest glossy that saw its way into the world every Saturday, and would I like to write a column for it? It would only be 610 words, but it would be the end-of-the-mag funny column and I could write about anything I liked.

Anything I liked! This was the job I had been waiting for all my life. Reviewing things is fine, and it gives me opportunities other journalism wouldn't, but this was a different sort of opportunity, to see what I was really capable of. I didn't know, and to be honest neither did Simon, so it was brave of him to give me a go.

Initially I thought the word count would be a problem. I thought eight hundred would have been nice, would have given me more space to let rip. But 610 has disciplines all its own. You have to get in quick, get out more quickly and you aren't there for long. Every sentence has to count. I have always preferred concision anyway. If this book were twice as long, would it be twice as good, or just twice as long?

I am proud of these pieces as I am proud of almost nothing else in my career. The *Independent* was coming to the end of its thirty-year life as a proper newspaper, printed on real paper with real ink, so almost no one read any of them, other than my friends and family, and even some of them I had to pay. But I don't care. Good work is its own reward, and if wealth, fame and acclaim don't follow as a matter of course, so what? (And if you believe that you'll believe anything.)

> To the Essex coast, to watch my cricket team in action. I have barely played this season, for all sorts of reasons: knee injury, then too much work, then mild depression, then too much work again, then ankle injury. I sustained this last one on my doorstep after a jolly evening, and should have put some ice on it straightaway. But no, I thought, it's only a twisted ankle, it'll be better in the morning. Six weeks later, I am still hobbling about.
>
> But if I can't play, I can watch, I can score, maybe do a little umpiring. It's not that I add much to the team when I actually play. I don't bowl, having retired from that discipline in 1985 after an over that included nine wides. I bat low in the order, and some would say it's not low enough. I can stop the ball in the field, and I take more catches than I drop, but I can't throw for toffee. Cricket has a way of throwing a spotlight on incompetence. You can carry a donkey or two in a football team, but in cricket even the least perspicacious batsman will spot the useless fielder, and hit every shot in his direction.

You can run, but you can't hide. In our team, most of us can't even run.

We have aged together. Earlier in the season I totted up everyone's ages and worked out that the XI had an aggregate age of 604 years. You should see our fielding practices before the game. Passing motorists slow down to stare, as they would for a unusually spectacular accident on a motorway.

This Essex game is one of our favourites, mainly because they like us and 'get' us, and also because they have an unusually benign microclimate, so it's usually warmer and drier there than everywhere else. But the other reason we all queue up to play this game is that the hosts always lay on an enormous dinner afterwards. More than cricket, possibly more than life itself, my teammates like food.

We win the toss and choose to field first, to build up a proper appetite for tea. The hosts score 179 before declaring. Among the highlights of their innings are two run outs, one of them perpetrated by Francis, who has become rather stately in the field. But not, on this occasion, as stately as the batsman.

Our opening batsmen wander out after consuming a pile of scones. Simon, the more nervous of the two, is aware that he is on forty-nine career ducks, mainly because Tim just told him. Three balls later Simon is out for 0, bowled by a young woman who looks about twelve. She turns out to be twenty and the best bowler on either side. Back in the pavilion we are wondering who in our team today is most like Captain Mainwaring in *Dad's Army*. It's a tricky one, but everyone agrees I am Sgt Wilson. Simon, whose entire philosophy of life could be summed up by the phrase 'Don't panic!', is Lance

Corporal Jones. Half of the rest of them are Private Fraser, the other half are Private Godfrey.

Cometh the hour, cometh the man. With an over to go, and four to win, last man Francis strides out to the crease. But he is a decent batsman, batting at eleven because he is in a strop. He hits the required boundary and strides back. It is our fourth victory in sixteen games, an incredibly high proportion for us. The sizzle of incipient barbecue greets the returning fielders.

You don't need to die to go to heaven. If you can avoid the roadworks, it's just a short drive down the A12.

19 September 2015

———

Danger lies everywhere. Deadly peril stalks the land. We cannot relax for a second. Even confectionery has it in for us.

Or so I discovered the other day, as I sat in an office I occasionally borrow for a book I am working on.* The project involves much reading of dusty binders full of old magazines, which normally live several floors below this office. I sit and read and eat sandwiches, taking care not to spatter semi-chewed food over this unique archive. Once the sandwiches are gone I move onto the sweeties, and it was while I was idly nibbling a chocolate raisin that I felt something a little crunchy in my mouth. Too crunchy for comfort, in fact. As I felt around inside my mouth with my tongue, I realised that one of my molars was rather smaller than it had been a minute earlier, and now had razor-sharp edges.

---

*   *The Spectator Book of Wit, Humour and Mischief* (2016).

What to do? First, there was some panicking to be done, and from there I moved swiftly on to rage, disappointment and remorse. After the age of fifty we know that our teeth are vulnerable and fragile, and they will only get worse. We floss and brush incessantly to try and make up for not having flossed and brushed enough before. And still the little bastards crack and crumble, even when presented with something as harmless as a chocolate raisin. A few years ago I had to forswear wine gums (which I can still taste, with the sweet tooth of my imagination) after one of them dislodged a gold tooth on a train just outside Wareham. 'Ah, wine gums,' said the dentist the following day, shaking her head sagely. 'Not quite as dangerous as fruit pastilles, but close.'

After shock and shame, then, came nameless dread, for the only thing worse than pain is the fear of pain to come. The tooth didn't hurt yet, but it would: the only question was when. It was Friday afternoon. Of course it was! Teeth only ever break five minutes after your dentist has gone home for the weekend. I rang up and, after some judicious begging, secured an emergency appointment for first thing Tuesday morning. Three days and four nights away. What were the most powerful painkillers we had in the house? Would it be acceptable to weep pitifully in front of the children?

In the event, the tooth only throbbed intermittently. A more acute problem was the tongue, which couldn't avoid Edward Scissortooth if it tried. Within twenty-four hours it was like having a sore duvet in your mouth. Talking was agony. Which was good news for everyone, as the only thing I wanted to talk about was my tooth.

On Saturday night I dreamt vivid dreams of Blu-tack, and on Sunday morning I found a blob and stuck it over the offending gnasher. It worked superbly. The tongue calmed down and as long as I remembered to take out the Blu-tack whenever I ate or drank, I was fine. Over the next forty-eight hours I inadvertently swallowed so much of the stuff you could have hung posters up with me, but I don't think there were any lasting effects.

On Tuesday morning the dentist told me she had never seen such a small crack on a tooth. Instead of the thousands of pounds of reconstructive surgery I had feared, she repaired it in five minutes without anaesthetic. Afterwards she said I'd been very brave and gave me a sticker. I felt proud as I left her surgery, and oddly ready for whatever life might throw at me next. A packet of chocolate peanuts seemed the obvious way to celebrate.

26 September 2015

———

I don't drive, so when I'm playing for my oldsters cricket team I usually beg a lift from one of two teammates who live nearby. But on this particular Sunday neither was playing, so I ventured down to the badlands of Highbury to get a lift from Tim, our incredibly angry fast bowler, who is no longer fast but still incredibly angry. Tim drives down motorways at the speed of a V2 rocket, beeping dawdlers and deploying the middle finger for anyone who hogs the middle lane.

'Where's the map?' I asked, for although I am no driver, I am a navigator of rare skill and acuity.

'Just behind you,' said Tim.

'I don't think this is going to be much help.'

'Why not?' said Tim, irritably.

'It's a map of France.'

Still, we had satnav and a postcode, and we reached our Suffolk destination eventually, for satnav, I find, is unequalled in finding and recommending the seventh or eighth fastest route anywhere, even to the end of the road. If I'd had a map, we'd have got there much more quickly. Possibly before we'd left, with Tim at the wheel.

Several hours later, after squeaking a slightly ill-tempered draw against much younger and better opposition, it was time to go home. On this occasion I blagged a lift from Tom, who was going to see his girlfriend, who lives not far from me. Tom had a shiny new car, and satnav, and no map. Who needs a map these days? Old technology.

There was a diversion outside the village, and we didn't really know where we were anyway, so Tom followed the satnav's instructions, while Alex, the other passenger, and I drivelled inconsequentially. There had nearly been a fist-fight during our team's innings, so there was much to discuss.

Half an hour later, having anatomised the parlous state of current pop music, we found ourselves in a town, in a traffic jam. Where were we? Tom wound the window down and asked. The man in the hi-vis jacket looked at us pityingly. We were in Sudbury, and the centre of the town was closed because a substantial chunk of it appeared to be burning down.

How were we to get out? The man in the hi-vis jacket recommended that road over there, so we took that. The satnav kept telling us to go back the way we had come. After six miles or so of this nagging, we gave in, turned round and went back.

'No, that's definitely the way you want to go,' said the same man in the hi-vis jacket, whose integrity we were beginning to doubt. But every route we tried, the satnav eventually led us back to the same roundabout, often by the most circuitous of routes. We had no mobile coverage, so could not raise a map by those means. It was like an episode of *The Prisoner*. Every wrong turning we took, we expected a huge white barrage balloon to head us off.

Eventually, at a bleak and abandoned roundabout, we chanced upon an unusually sad McDonald's. Even the happier ones are quite miserable, but this was the black dog of fast food joints. We stopped there and munched hamburgers in gloomy silence. There was nothing more to be said, possibly ever.

Finally we escaped, found a mobile signal, sourced a map. It took us three and a quarter hours to get home. Tom rang his girlfriend to check she was awake, and woke her up. He wouldn't be going round there tonight after all.

I have bought a map. Hooray for old technology.

10 October 2015

———

A friend of mine has developed an unhealthy obsession with cheesestrings – for let's face it, there can be no other kind. One cheesestring is never enough. Three, you die. My friend has been under a lot of stress recently. She has small children who crave cheesestrings even more than she does. But her self-control in always managing to keep herself down to two cheesestrings in any one four-hour period has been exemplary.

Far too much is written about food that everyone wants to eat: nice food, healthy food, full of 'fresh ingredients' locally sourced from Sainsbury's. Nowhere near enough is written about the food that people actually eat, whether they want to or not, whether they admit it or not. As a longtime resident of north London, I am sure I am not alone in feeling a tiny prickle of shame when I go to the shop up the road and buy a Dr Oetker pizza for lunch. Are there no 'Pollo' ones left? Then a 'Spinaci' it will have to be. With teenage children in the flat, I can pretend that I am buying it for them, that they will eat it with their friends in eleven seconds flat. And that this family-sized tub of Carte d'Or ice cream (with real strawberry pieces) isn't entirely for me either. But the shop's owners are not fooled. They have seen me salivating over the Rolo desserts in their chiller cabinet. (Now on special offer! Four for the price of two! That's two to eat right now, and two more to eat in a few minutes' time!)

They have witnessed me at the zenith of my cravings for Heinz Baked Beans with Pork Sausages. Is there really pork in those sausages? How do they manage to taste unlike real sausages and yet exactly the same as the 'sausages' in every previous tin I have opened? My school had what was rather pretentiously called a 'dining hall', and it was a ten-minute walk from the main school buildings. And on the way there lurked a hot dog van, which we pupils had been strongly discouraged from patronising. It was dirty, we were told. You didn't know where those sausages had been. There were queues ten deep every day. The rubbery, taste-free hot dogs, of unknown provenance. The snowy-white buns, ominously chalky in texture. And the tomato ketchup, whose manufacture had surely bypassed the tomato altogether. It was disgusting. It was delicious. I want one now.

Alcohol should probably be mentioned at this point, for booze can affect our taste buds, much as it does our conversation, digestion, libido and lives. When not in the pub I quite enjoy a salted peanut or two. But after a few sharpeners, dry roasted peanuts, with their distinctive taste of chemicals and physical ruin, come into their own. You can feel them stripping the lining from your throat as you swallow them. And yet nothing else will do.

Once, a long time ago, a newspaper executive took me out to lunch and sounded me out about becoming their restaurant critic. I had to come clean. Much as I love posh food, especially when I'm not paying for it, my true tastes could not be concealed forever. Sooner or later the mask would slip, and I would have to admit that instead of this *tarte fine aux pommes avec crème anglaise*, I'd rather be at home with my head stuck in an enormous bowl of butterscotch-flavoured Angel Delight. The executive stared into space for a few seconds, possibly remembering the long-discontinued mint chocolate flavour, and then we moved on to talk about something else.

7 November 2015

—

The tall blonde woman with whom I share this flat, a queen-sized bed and a familiar creeping anxiety about where our teenage children have got to, stepped in something nasty the other day. She often goes for a health-restoring amble on Hampstead Heath, which has long since become a sort of vast, extended dog toilet, attracting incontinent canines and their gleeful owners from miles around. I knew something of the sort had happened when I came home and saw the offending boot on the doorstep. She hates having to clean poo off her shoes, as who doesn't? One of the most marvellous moments in a parent's life is when you realise you have wiped your children's bottoms for the last time. Not only can they now do it for themselves, they prefer to, and you are officially off the hook. Years later you might feel slightly sentimental about this and remember this turd removal duty with a certain nostalgic fondness. But you will be wearing rose-tinted spectacles, as well as a rose-coloured peg on your nose.

As I write, the boot is out there still. It's only five days, but the tall blonde woman figures that no one is likely to steal a single boot, especially if it is tainted with the muck of hounds. Out of sight, though, means out of mind. When she goes in and out of the house, I don't think she even sees it. Buddhist monks practise mind control techniques for decades to reach this state of grace. I could offer to clean the boot myself, but obviously I'm not going to do that.

The thing is, it's not the first time this has happened. The other night I was coming back from the pub with my friend and neighbour Alan, who spotted the solitary footwear item immediately. 'The return of the poo shoe,' he said, portentously. It's not actually the same one: the previous incumbent was a daggy old trainer that sat on the step for a while, about a year ago. 'Do you remember that, then?' I said. 'The poo shoe?' said Alan. 'Of course. Everybody remembers the poo shoe.' I thought it had been there for a couple of weeks, maybe a month at most, but Alan said it had sat there for at least three months. 'Funny,' I said, 'you never mentioned it.' 'Well you don't,' said Alan, miming a telephone call. 'Hello Marcus, it's Alan. How are you? And did you know that there's a shoe with poo on it that has been sitting on your doorstep for a quarter of a year?'

Apparently the shoe had become something of a local

cause célèbre. Some of our neighbours began to find its presence oddly reassuring. Its apparent permanence contrasted favourably with the constant change and disruption of everyday city life. Go out in the morning to work, pass the poo shoe. Come back home that evening, poo shoe still there.

She did clean it eventually, of course, by which time its doggy contribution had dried to a fine powder. It didn't even smell any more. I am not sure the shoe was strictly wearable after it had been out in all weathers. But Alan said that people missed it. They wondered what had happened. For them this was a story that hadn't ended satisfactorily: it had just stopped, in the middle of the last chapter, without explanation. I had no idea of any of this.

And now there is a poo boot out there. Word is getting round. Tourists will soon be flocking. Perhaps we should charge admission. 10p to look, 50p to touch, £5 to clean the boot.

8 January 2016

Could I have kept this up? I don't know. I'd like to think so; but to be honest I suspect not. After all, almost no one can. When I was putting together my book for the *Spectator*, I read an awful lot of columns by an awful lot of columnists. It was a little like a masterclass in the art of writing a column, especially the sort of first-person stuff that I like doing. And while many columnists started with a surge of energy and ideas, almost none of them could maintain quality control for more than a year or two. Once you have exhausted all the weird and wacky things that have actually happened to you, where do you go? To the weird and wacky things that have happened to people you know and then, finally, to the weird and wacky things that might have happened to you if you weren't busy all the time writing. I'm not saying everyone makes it up, but I bet a few do, and I understand why. What's the choice?

Writers don't like giving up columns. It feels like an own goal, an unforced error, and when you do it (as I have done a couple of times) people give you funny looks. It's almost as though you are letting the side down. This is what editors are for, of course, but many favour a quiet life that doesn't involve finding new columnists to replace the perfectly decent ones they already have. And the fact is that readers take so long to start liking a column that some columnists only achieve popularity when they have already started to go off. Columnists are a little like cheese: you tend to notice the ones that smell the most, but not necessarily for the right reasons.

My *Independent* column lasted just thirty weeks before the paper ceased to exist as anything other than a sorry website. Simon, all the staff, all the contributors and I were given the boot. They had lost their jobs; I had just lost a column; so there was a limit to the amount I could publicly mourn. But even so. Beyond the unspeakable sadness, I tried to rationalise this latest disaster. It's not as though I hadn't been sacked before, and it's not as though I won't be sacked again. There's a good reason that all freelances fear the chop, because the chop is waiting around the next corner, sniggering evilly, as chops tend to.

16

Lessons

'Writing is really a way of thinking – not just feeling,
but thinking about things that are disparate, unresolved,
mysterious, problematic or just sweet.'

Toni Morrison

Why do we write, any of us? My friend Kate, who produces magical children books and not appreciably less magical novels for adults too, has narrative pouring out of her. She thinks of stories as the rest of us exhale. The Belgian novelist Georges Simenon produced several hundred short novels in a forty-year career, including seventy-five featuring Inspector Maigret. Look at one of his novels and count the chapters. If there are eleven chapters, it took him eleven days to write. After bashing out a Maigret, he needed a good lie-down, but after he had produced one of his much bleaker *romans durs*, he had to absent himself from all civilisation for a fortnight and sometimes became quite ill. He wasn't doing it for fun. *He had no choice.*

When I was younger I wrote because I could, because I had things to say, because it was my career, and because I was extremely ambitious. Which of these apply now? It seems to me that the main reason why I write now – and this is going to sound awfully pretentious – is to establish the truth. That's the truth about the book or film I am reviewing, the truth about the world, the truth about the way people behave, the truth about myself. I realise that I'm constantly looking for the thing that no one else has said, but only if it has meaning, if it has resonance. There's no point coming up with something original if it also happens to be complete drivel. Obviously, as writers, we are often wrong, and we accept that. We may not actually be very good at seeking the truth, but we are sincere in our search. And there's nothing more satisfying than coming up with a wholly original thought that happens to be indisputably right. It just doesn't happen very often.

In the same way, writers are frequently asked where they get their ideas from, and of course most of them haven't a clue. 'Just out of the sightline' would probably be my own answer. Think of life as the vista in front of you. If you don't move your head too far, that vista ranges for about 180 degrees, from far left to far right. The best ideas never come from straight ahead. They always come out of the margins, barely visible at first, and it's only when you see them and grab them and make them your own do they really start to make sense. The crucial thing is that these ideas never seem to be your own. They just appear, presumably out of your subconscious. The best writers are those who can recognise the good ideas from the bad ideas, and know what to do with them when they manifest themselves.

I'm not one of the best writers by a long chalk, but compiling this book has shown me that I have a voice, that it's unusual and distinctive, and that I probably always had it, right from the beginning, when I was teaching myself to write. Not every writer needs such a voice; indeed, for many it would be an intrusion. Someone like Craig Brown, a parodist of rare gifts, or Miles Kington, a hero of mine, don't or didn't have strong voices. They suborned their gifts to the task in hand, which in both cases meant writing huge numbers of wonderful words that made hundreds of thousands of people laugh most days of the week. A strong voice in either case could be seen as a prison, because it limits you to writing only certain things; but at the same time, mine has given me a career, for which I remain pathetically grateful.

This is my eleventh book in just over twenty-five years. My original plan was to make it a combination of what publishers call a Professional Confessional (person who works at a job tells you what it's really like) and a Greatest Hits of Journalism, with the emphasis on the latter. I found an enormous cardboard box in the loft which had most of my cuttings from my first ten years. I started to go through the box with some gusto, picking out pieces I enjoyed and retyping the best bits. But more quickly than I expected, this began to pall. Who cares about TV reviews of forgotten programmes from twenty-five years ago? Of the 457 TV reviews I wrote for the *Daily Mail* between 1989 and 1996, excerpts selected only from the first hundred appear in this book. Even then, I have cut down massively on what I first included. With each successive draft, more pieces have gone. Slash and burn! Slash and burn!

So I had thought, rather arrogantly, that my journalism was special and that it was bound to have survived, and I found, rather more humbly, that however special it might have seemed at the time, much of it now sits on the page like a dead dog. I have always felt a bit sorry for political columnists, who write cogently and authoritatively about what's going on, only to find that events change everything and what they wrote yesterday matters not at all today. But it turns out that this is equally true of droll reviewers of TV, film, books and pop music. I have written many millions of words these past thirty-five years for newspapers and magazines, and if we discount the bills they paid, I might never have bothered. Oddly enough, I find this more comforting than disturbing. After all, I enjoyed writing them at the time and they did pay an awful lot of bills, and to expect anything more than that is to expect too much.

This is why so many journalists drift away from the daily grind and start writing books, firstly to rescue themselves from the stress of constant deadlines, but also because they feel that books will form a more permanent testament to their genius. This, too, might be an illusion. Take J. B. Priestley. A hugely famous, rich and prolific writer and novelist in his lifetime, Priestley has simply vanished from bookshops and libraries since his death. The only works of his that survive are a couple of plays he wrote that are occasionally revived: *An Inspector Calls* and *When We Are Married*. I am quite fond of a little book of his called *Delight*, a series of droll little essays about things and places that please him, but has anyone under fifty read his novels? Anyone at all?

Posterity will surely be denied to most of us, although to be fair I'm not sure why someone like me should expect future generations of readers to pay me or my contemporaries a blind bit of notice. There will be future generations of bitter and impoverished writers queueing up for their attention, and the best of luck to them.

So this book started out as roughly three-quarters Greatest Hits of Journalism and a quarter Professional Confessional, and changed in the writing to the precise opposite. It has been great fun to write, not least because many of the stories and ideas I have put in have been bouncing around the inside of my head for years, with nowhere else to go. But it has also been useful because I am sixty-one and so no longer young, even though I have nearly all my own teeth and my knees don't yet creak audibly when I'm going upstairs. As W. Somerset Maugham, another whose reputation has declined since death, once wrote,

... it occurred to me that the greatest compensation of old age is its freedom of spirit.

I suppose that is accompanied by a certain indifference to many of the things that men in their prime think important. Another compensation is that it liberates you from envy, hatred and malice. I do not believe that I envy anyone. I have made the most of such gifts as nature provided me with; I do not envy the greater gifts of others. I have had a great deal of success. I do not envy the success of others ... I no longer mind what people think of me. They can take me or leave me.

Maugham was older than me, richer than me, more famous than me and probably drunker than me when he wrote that, but I feel similarly. It's for this reason that there isn't much settling of scores in this book. Partly this is because I don't feel quite so angry about things as I used to, and because I know now that there's no point taking such things personally. But it's also because my old friend Harry Thompson, when he was grievously ill with lung cancer, wrote a book called *Penguins Stopped Play*, about his cricket team's round-the-world trip. That book sold more than all my books put together, because he was by then quite well known, and because he died just before it was published, which gave the book a terrible and sad ending that really resonated with readers. It's also very funny and well observed. But if you knew him at all well, the book was more upsetting for the large number of untruths it contained and his brutal judgements of people who had thought they were his friends until they read what he had written about them. I know he was an angry man when he wrote it, angry at the dreadful unfairness of his illness. But fifteen years on, there are still a dozen or so people who remember Harry with no great fondness for what he said about them in that book. I think that's a shame, and I have long wondered whether being ruled by such fury and loathing was what gave him his cancer in the first place.* It just seems no way to live your life, and no way to die your death.

Being freed from envy and ambition, though, feels like an unexpected stroke of luck, and I wrote a lot about this in my book about middle age, *A Shed of One's Own*. When I was young I felt I was competing with everyone, which felt horrible and didn't even work, as these were never competitions I was going to win. There are always people more talented than you, better connected than you, cleverer than you, richer than you. I had dinner a while ago with a friend who must be worth, at a conservative guess, £15 million. He got a little drunk and revealed that he was mortally jealous of a mutual friend of ours, who is probably worth £25 million. I said not a thing and left him to his pain.

Some things you can control and most you simply can't. I say, control the ones you can and forget about the others. Most writers, whether competing or not, are in the same boat, one with a very small hole in it, far from shore. We have to make connections with each other, or we're sunk. Some writers stare at you, like Marcel Berlins on *Round Britain Quiz*, trying to identify whether or not you are a threat. I believe I am a threat to nothing and no one, but nowadays I tend to stare back, pretending to be a threat, and funnily enough they usually prefer that, because reinforcing their own prejudices makes them feel safer than engaging with the enemy. Which may make sense in your twenties, when it's you against the world, but is pretty feeble in your fifties and sixties, when it's us against the world, or nothing.

As writers we are unusually susceptible to the whims and favours of editors, and becoming more so as fees are reduced and money once used to pay for writing is redirected to the capacious pockets of chief executives. In my experience, you can still build a decent freelance career on the support of four or five 'patrons',

---

* It certainly wasn't smoking. Harry never smoked a cigarette in his life.

people who like your work and, moreover, are willing to employ you to do some. If it hadn't been for Jenny Naipaul at the *Spectator*, where would I be now? She feels confident that I would have made it anyway, without her help, but I can't honestly imagine how.

We need our luck and we need our patrons. When one patron is sacked or, worse, turns up his or her toes, you will feel the lack nearly as much as he or she does. Almost every time I have lost a job I valued, it's because an editor who liked my stuff was replaced by an editor who didn't. I'm not complaining. It's just the way it is, and the more times it happens to you the more stoically you can accept it, as you bang your forehead on the wall until it bleeds.

I don't think I could have written a book like this ten years ago. Mellowness is hard won, and one of the primary benefits of getting older, if you're lucky. Some of my contemporaries are becoming more and more deranged as they age: angrier, more miserable, more thwarted, and more apt to have flecks of foam adorning the sides of their lips. These are dangerous years, but I think it has helped my mental health no end to be still working as a writer, and specifically, writing this book, which I now see has been a form of therapy, and much cheaper than the usual sort. The red wine helps, too. The red wine always helps.

Afterword: Love and Work

I finished this book in February 2020, just as Covid-19 was rolling up its sleeves and getting to work. We were planning to publish in early 2021, but in the summer of 2020 I asked the publishers to delay it a while. The lockdown months were grim and challenging, and *How to Be a Writer* suddenly seemed too sunny a book for its times. I am at heart an optimist, and rereading the book now, six months later, I have realised that it is actually this optimism that has fuelled my career and life and kept me going through the tougher phases. But 2020 was not an optimistic year. It was frightening, it was frustrating, and even a 24-carat introvert like me struggled with the restrictions, especially after Dominic Cummings took his drive to Barnard Castle to test his eyesight. (I would have been tempted to poke them out and see what he thought of that.)

What to do? Graham Gouldman, once of 10cc, called one of his later albums *Love and Work*, the implication being that once you get to a certain age, that's really all that matters. I had my family around me in the small flat we still seem to share, bickering with each other constantly, but there was still work, and fortunately I had a book to write. This was *Berkmann's Pop Miscellany*, which I started and finished during lockdown, not because I had suddenly become a Jedi master of productivity, but because there was literally nothing else to do.

In the early days of lockdown we weren't allowed to go outside other than to take exercise or queue outside Sainsbury's. Sitting down on a bench in your local park was expressly outlawed, on pain of death. On my long walks through the local green spaces, I found a corner of one park that no one ever walked through or past, that was surrounded by magnificent old trees and, because there was no traffic on the roads, was wonderfully peaceful and serene. I would go and sit on the ground under some trees for an hour or more and read a book. If I had been caught I would no doubt still be in some dungeon somewhere, being whipped every hour on the hour, but these quiet times probably saved my sanity. I found I could not read anything that was too emotionally taxing, that contained too much peril or risk. The warm comfort blankets of P. G. Wodehouse, Barbara Pym and Simenon's Maigret novels seemed far more appropriate.

Work became a bubble into which I could escape every morning for a few hours. Time seemed to speed up. As I was making the bed I would think, is it only twenty-four hours since I last did this? Twenty-four hours later, I would think, is it only twenty-four hours since I last thought, is it only twenty-four hours since I last did this? On the other side of the road there is a man (and I'm assuming it's a man as I have never seen him) who has a huge widescreen TV on his wall and appears to watch it day and night. Once I woke up for a pee at half past five, looked out of the window and he still had it on.

People were terrified. In the years to come we must try not to forget how frightened people were, convinced that the plague was upon us and that if we caught it we would surely die. Living in London, I caught it early, and had it only mildly. When I got better, I told my friends that I had had it and many did not believe me because I was still alive. I would meet people in the street, tell them I had had it and every one of them, every single one of them, took a step back inadvertently. Three months after I had had it, when I was clearly not infectious and almost certainly immune, a friend of mine refused to give me a lift to cricket matches in case he caught it off me. I offered to wear a mask and sit in the back seat with the windows open, but no.

That's not to say that much of the fear wasn't justified. A friend of a friend in his seventies, a doctor, caught the lurgy very early and was proper poorly, but recovered. Asked what difference the disease had made, he said, I'm still alive but I know for certain that it has abbreviated my life: I shan't live as long as I was hoping to. My friend Russell, who is the same age as me and of similar build and temperament, had cancer a few years ago, from which he recovered after radiotherapy. When he caught Covid-19, he was in hospital for four and a half weeks and was still suffering after-effects six months later, with no end in sight.

'What doesn't kill you makes you stronger': what nonsense. What doesn't kill you may eat away at you in all sorts of ways you hadn't expected. I thought, rather blithely, that having spent the last thirty years working from home and avoiding humanity as much as possible, a few more months of the same would be relatively easy for me. Parties would be cancelled, pubs and restaurants would be closed but the disease would soon be vanquished and everything would be back to normal sooner or later. But as the months dragged on, I began to miss my friends terribly. I missed the sheer fun of social interaction. The long boozy lunches. The adventure of a party where you might not know anyone. The making of new friends. Work started to pall. I finished the *Pop Miscellany* and quickly realised how *tired* I was. Tired to the bone and beyond. Even when pubs and restaurants reopened, I had many friends who would still not leave their homes, and I could understand that. After a while you become institutionalised. A trip to the shops, some-thing previously routine, now becomes a supreme effort. There were times when I had to go to the post office up the road and it took me three or four days to summon up the energy.

One of the weirder things about being a writer is that you can lose confidence in some of your books without even going to the effort of rereading them. Three nights ago I had a dream in which I reread one of my less successful books, and discovered that I had included, as an appendix, several pages of a fashion catalogue with loads of grinning male models wearing cashmere cardigans. When I woke up I actually had to check that this wasn't so. As the writing of *How to Be a Writer* receded into a distant, disease-free past, I decided that it was smug and self-satisfied and way too pleased with itself, and that sooner or later I would have to reread it and thoroughly de-smug it before publication. So I reread the book yesterday and was astonished to find that it wasn't smug at all. (You may disagree, of course.) I realised too that I had been completely wrong to pull it from the schedules in terror that it would be poorly received. But that's the writer's temperament all over: often ridiculous over-confidence tempered by equally ludicrous hyper-sensitivity. I have a writer friend who believes that her first novel, published more than twenty years ago, is still blighted by a single vicious review it received from an important newspaper. It is, but only in her mind. (It's a pretty good novel.) My guess is that there's not a single other person alive who has any memory of this, even the person who wrote the review.

She will get her revenge, though. Don't be in the slightest doubt about that. She is a writer.

October 2020

Acknowledgements

Cliff Allen, Paul Bajoria, Louis Barfe, Peter Bently, James Berkmann, Martha Berkmann, Jean Berkmann-Barwis, Richard Beswick, Paula Bingham, John Boden, Thomas Coops, Rhiannon Coslett, Sam Craft, Lucy Curtin, Alan and Selena Doggett-Jones, Susie Dowdall, Matthew Engel, Sally Farrimond, Sally Ann Fitt, Maisie Glazebrook, Joanna Green, Natalie Gregorian, Zoe Gullen, Ian Hislop, Corinna Honan, Rachel Hore, Sarah Jackson, Mark Jacobs, David Jaques, Bob Jones, Aalia Khan, Nicholas Lezard, Veronica Marris, Andrew Martin, Mark Mason, Lucy Maycock, Roger Morgan-Grenville, Sally Morris, Jenny Naipaul, Nick Newman, Paul Noakes, Simon O'Hagan, Georgia Pairtrie, Julian Parker, Sandra Parsons, Francis Peckham, Neal Ransome, Tina Roche, Patrick Routley, Terence Russoff, Richard Spence, Mitchell Symons, D. J. Taylor, Russell Taylor, Pat Thomas, Bethen Thorpe, Patrick Walsh, Francis Wheen, Alan White, Robert Wilson.

This book is dedicated to my fellow writers and lunchers Kate Saunders and Amanda Craig, with whom I meet up every few weeks for a 'works outing' at which we complain about everything, and to our occasional guest Jane Thynne, who was the first person I told the idea for this book, at a party years ago, and who reacted with such enthusiasm I became convinced it was an idea of brilliance even though no one else thought it was. The fact that I can't remember whose party it was, where it was held or anything else that happened there is a testament to the robustness of the writerly ego we all share.

Credits

Extracts from articles by the author originally appeared in the *Spectator*, the *Daily Mail*, *Private Eye*, *Punch*, the *Oldie*, the *Independent* and the *Independent on Sunday*.

'Winning by a shorn head' and 'All the booze that's fit to sprint' (Punch Cartoon Library/TopFoto) reproduced by permission of TopFoto.

With thanks to *Private Eye*, notably Ian Hislop and Sheila Molnar, for permission to reprint contributions to the magazine.

1   Patrick Campbell, *My Life and Easy Times* (London: Anthony Blond, 1967)

5   Virginia Woolf, *Orlando* (London: Hogarth Press, 1968)

33   Lisa Allardice, 'Kate Atkinson: "I live to entertain. I don't live to teach or preach or to be political"', *Guardian*, 15 June 2019

39, 103 Suzanne Moore, 'Find a room of your own: top 10 tips for women who want to write', *Guardian*, 5 October 2019

49   Gary Younge, 'In these bleak times, imagine a world where you can thrive', *Guardian*, 10 January 2020

61   Edward Gorey, *The Unstrung Harp: Or, Mr Earbrass Writes a Novel* (New York: Duell, Sloan and Pearce, 1953)

62   Samuel Beckett, 'Worstward Ho' (1983)

71   www.twitter.com/jenniferemorrow, 27 December 2019. Reproduced by kind permission of Jennifer Morrow

81   Fran Lebowitz, 'Letters', *The Fran Lebowitz Reader* (London: Virago, 2021)

95   Alasdair Gray, *Lanark: A Life in Four Books* (Edinburgh: Canongate, 1981)

107*   Nicholas Lezard. 'While trying to avoid a deadline, I come across a novelist who sells 27 books every minute', *New Statesman*, 1 December 2014

143   Leonora Carrington, *The Hearing Trumpet* (Paris: Flammarion, 1974)

147   Neil Gaiman in *Write* (London: Guardian Books, 2012)

149   Harry Fieldhouse, *Everyman's Good English Guide* (London: Everyman, 1982)

153   Gore Vidal, interview in *Paris Review* (1981)

167   Keith Waterhouse, quoted in *Independent*, 1 March 1999

181   Toni Morrison, in Sybil Steinberg (ed.), *Writing for Your Life* (Wainscott: Pushcart Press, 1992)

185   W. Somerset Maugham, *A Writer's Notebook* (London: William Heinemann, 1949)